English Studies 11–18

An arts-based approach

edited by

Bernard T. Harrison

HODDER AND STOUGHTON
LONDON SYDNEY AUCKLAND TORONTO

British Library Cataloguing in Publication Data

English studies, 11–18: an arts-based approach.
  1. English language——Study and teaching
  I. Harrison, Bernard T.
  428   LB1631
ISBN 0 340 33157 7

First published 1983

Typeset by Wyvern Typesetting Ltd, Bristol in 11/12 point Palatino (Linotron)
Printed in Great Britain for Hodder and Stoughton Educational, a division of Hodder
and Stoughton Ltd, Mill Road, Dunton Green, Sevenoaks, Kent by Robert Hartnoll, Ltd,
Bodmin, Cornwall.

Contents

Notes on Contributors

Bernard T. Harrison has been Head of an English Department in a London Comprehensive School and now lectures in English and Education in the Division of Education, University of Sheffield. He is the author of *Learning through Writing* (1983).

Peter Clough has taught English in comprehensive and special schools; he is currently writing a phenomenological account of language, based on his observations of the quality of pupils' classroom talk in English studies.

Peter Abbs lectures in English and Education in the School of Education, University of Sussex. Recent publications include *Reclamations* (1979) and *English Within the Arts* (1982).

Alan England has been Head of an English Department in a Liverpool Comprehensive School, and now lectures in Drama and Education in the Division of Education, University of Sheffield. He is the author of *Scripted Drama: A Practical Guide to Teaching Techniques* (1981).

Bernadette Walsh teaches English and Drama in a Sheffield Comprehensive School, and has special responsibility for pastoral care; she is engaged on research into the quality of language provision for 'remedial' learners.

Helen and Colin Pearce teach English and Drama in Sheffied Comprehensive Schools.

David Allen has been Head of two English Departments in Sheffield Comprehensive Schools; has worked as Curriculum Development Officer in English for the City of Sheffield; and is now Inspector for English in Nottinghamshire. He is the author of *English Teaching since 1965: How Much Growth?* (1980).

John M. P. Hodgson teaches English in a Devon Comprehensive School. He has been Head of English in a Leicestershire Community College/School.

Malcolm Stanton is Head of English in a Derbyshire Comprehensive School.

John Brown lectures in English and Drama at Bretton Hall College of Education. He was engaged in the Schools Council English 16–19 Project.

Terry Gifford is Head of English in a Sheffield Comprehensive School. He is co-author with Neil Roberts of *Ted Hughes: A Critical Study* (1981).

Acknowledgments

We owe much to all those teachers, past and present, whose teachings have influenced our own efforts to realise the creative powers of language. We are grateful to all the pupils whose response and work have provided substance for these chapters. Special thanks are due to Mrs Sue Cramp, for her support and skill in helping to prepare and type this manuscript.

We stopped in the grove, beyond the threshing-floors, at the very end of the village. Semka picked up a stick from the snow and began to strike the frozen trunk of a linden tree. The hoarfrost fell from the branches upon his cap, and the lonely sound of his beating was borne through the forest.

Fedka said . . . 'Why do people learn singing? I often wonder why they really do?'

God knows what made him jump from the terrors of the murder to this question; but by everything, – by the sound of his voice, by the seriousness with which he requested an answer, but the silence which the other two preserved, – I could feel a vivid and lawful connection of this question and the preceding conversation . . .

'What is drawing for? And why is it good to write?' I said, positively not knowing how to explain to him what art was for.

'What is drawing for?' he repeated thoughtfully. What he was asking me was what was art for, and I did not dare and did not know how to explain to him . . . It seems strange to me to repeat what we spoke on that evening, but I remember we said everything, I think, that there ever was to be said on utility and on plastic and moral beauty.

Leo Tolstoy, *The School at Yasnaya Polyana*, 1862

Introduction

What is English for? Some Principal Issues

Bernard T. Harrison

This book is addressed to all teachers of English; in particular it has been compiled on behalf of those English teachers who are unwilling to submit their classes merely to a prison diet of course texts and exercises. We have aimed to include well-tried and practical advice from colleagues in the field, which might be adapted according to local needs and individual choices, to enhance the quality of school English studies. How can we plan and present a balanced, well-constructed plan of English work, which gives room to all essential aspects of English? Such a programme ought (obviously) to include all those language activities (talking, listening, reading, writing, drama) which we might reasonably expect that an English teacher should promote. It would include provision of fiction, poetry, plays, journals, tapes, videotapes, records, films and other texts and resources; and underpinning this programme will be a steady view of English as an art, as a creative discipline. Throughout these chapters there will be a trust held in the capacity of learners (as well as of teachers) to contribute creatively to the language(s) and culture(s) which they are studying to inherit.

We know how the vast majority of children, even those who may be seen by some of their teachers as having 'impoverished' or even 'no' language, come to school already equipped with voices that offer authentic reflections of their own varied individualities, their own locale, their own emergent views of living. Their individual idioms, tones and speech rhythms will reveal many subtle interactions between themselves and the world from which they receive, and to which they contribute. Our task as teachers lies in ensuring that this already vigorous exchange be further enriched and extended in the classroom. In order that their uses of language may be enhanced, our pupils need to be engaged – through enjoyment, and also through challenge – in the most interesting sources that are possible; for (to echo Dr Johnson on the subject of books) the English lesson is best justified according to how far it enables the better enjoying, and how far it enables the better enduring, of life's circumstances.

If acquiring language is a perfectly natural process (which would be hard to deny), formal English work can best be seen as offering creative extensions, and a creative discipline to a child's language through the creating and telling of stories, poems, plays and so on – in short, through art-discourse. To be able to attend without evasion to what we actually see and feel in the world, or to become aware of those more elusive feelings which still wait to be named, involves both a venturing and disciplining of imagination. This is the essence of what we term as artistic activity, in language or in other art-forms. But why should we make such an effort? Why should we all wish or even need to strive for new meanings? To the doubters we should dwell first, perhaps, on the enjoyableness of the initial venture – on the unstrained, celebratory, spontaneous aspects of creative activity. Creativity depends, in part, on the simplicity and insouciance of childhood itself:

> Art is childhood. Art means not to know that the world exists, and to make a world . . . A song, a picture which you treasure, a poem which you love, all this has its value and significance. I mean for him who creates it for the first time, and for him who creates it the second time; for the artist and for him who really appreciates.
>
> R. M. Rilke (*Werke*, VII, 280)

Our book can only be justified as a kind of spring-cleaning on behalf of English studies. It should aim to reaffirm to all teachers – the doubting, the steadfast, the weary and the enthusiastic – that the proper art of teaching the mother tongue is a worthwhile, satisfying task. If well done, their art brings essential benefit to every learner with whom they are in contact. It can also fulfil teachers' own needs, as beings who are themselves still learning and growing. For we cannot teach English well without being ourselves creatively involved, as co-makers of meaning. As teachers, we are bound up not only with learners, but *as* learners, through the weaving of learners' with teachers' experience, in the fabric of classroom discourse.

Of course, in seeking renewal, English teachers can draw from the roots of past good principles and practice, in order to enhance the quality of their own teaching. They may read Rilke's reflection on art and on childhood – now over half a century old – as an already slightly musty contribution from a past which may have believed, but without sufficient critical reflection, in the importance of 'art and creativity'. On the other hand, they may be disturbed, through experiencing some quickened sense of correspondence with Rilke's viewpoint. They may connect his sentences with their own intimations about the inestimable value of imaginative activity. The arts enable fresh statements, fresh visions of life; this could be the starting-point for a new approach, as it has been for English teachers in the past, from time to time.

With those needs in mind, the first three chapters of this book address themselves to three main areas of language activity. In the first chapter Peter Clough dwells on the need to give primary space to the learner's own talk in the classroom. Acknowledging the pathfinding work of Andrew Wilkinson, Douglas Barnes and others who have alerted teachers to ways in which learners think and learn through speaking, his view is that much remains still to be done, in order to enhance the quality of classroom talk. He provides a description, with substantial examples from his own classroom observations, of what actually happens when children are speaking and listening. In Chapter 2, Peter Abbs extends discussion about the nature of personal discourse through examples from the writings of his own students. He dwells on the essential importance of personal, autobiographical reflectiveness in both writing and reading, as the only sure way of developing a full focal understanding of new experience. Drawing from a wide range of sources, he advocates among other things the use of 'informal' literary material – from writers' diaries, letters, autobiographies, interviews, journals – in order to enable both teachers and learners to understand how the process of coming to know cannot be hurried; such methods will help to 'lift literature out of the museum and put it back in the market place'. In the third of these opening chapters, Alan England reveals, again with extensive classroom examples, the unique contribution that drama work can make to creative uses of language in English studies. These examples illuminate his concisely stated principles that drama work requires a continual interacting of enjoyment and discipline, of 'intensity of involvement and the understanding of the wholeness', of planned and unpredictable elements, to achieve its full impact.

In an important chapter on 'remedial' English work, Bernadette Walsh gives an account from her own teacher's notebook of work with a fourth year class of mixed backgrounds and origins, who have been lumped together as 'remedial'. She shows how, far from any 'watering down' of English provision to suit their own special needs, such children need even more than others to become fellow-explorers in richer landscapes of language. Some of the evidence presented in her chapter ought to raise fundamental questions about the nature of much 'remedial' provision at secondary level.

This chapter is followed by several accounts of planning and presenting different genres in the classroom. There are two on fiction, by Helen and Colin Pearce (younger forms) and by David Allen (fourth year). Both of these chapters manage to include descriptions of specific programmes of work, while also providing a fund of more general information about choices and approaches in the teaching of fiction. Helen and Colin Pearce dwell on the uses of the class reader, while David Allen's proposals emphasise the importance of pupils' choices in reading fiction. There would be value in selecting either (or both) of these chapters as a basis for discussion at, say, a departmental meeting where 'Approaches to Fiction' is on the agenda.

This was in fact a specific intention of the chapter on poetry teaching, where six points for planning, and six for the presenting of poetry are outlined. The huge topics that are introduced in these chapters all deserve far more space of course; but they are intended at least as direction-indicators, from which the reader may take an initiative for further work.

John Hodgson's chapter on the uses of film and television in English studies offers ample evidence from work in progress in his own teaching, that this is an area of essential importance for English studies. Avoiding exclusive 'either/or' positions ('film-as-art' versus 'visual literacy') he reveals the value of working both in terms of imaginative response to film and television, and of a more analytical study of the 'language' of film and television. The social awareness that guides this chapter becomes a major concern in Malcolm Stanton's contribution *Towards Public Issues*, which describes work with a CSE group. This chapter makes explicit what has been an underlying assumption of virtually all earlier chapters: that personal experience and artistic activity can never be seen in isolation from the wider concerns of the community; the one must always be embedded in the other, for the sake of individual and of cultural health.

Finally, Terry Gifford and John Brown show how the insights gained from imaginative English teaching up to 16+ need not be lost when 'A' level work is introduced. In a fitting conclusion to the book, these contributors give working examples of much that has been recommended in earlier chapters: the uses of informal (documentary) materials, as suggested by Peter Abbs; the value of engaging pupils in drama-in-performance; the possibilities of group work in poetry; and the uses of photographs, folk-songs and other artefacts, as suggested by Bernadette Walsh for her 'remedial' groups.

To reaffirm, as is our intent in this book, that language has fundamentally a poetic identity, is to draw on a long-held truth about the nature of language. The principle may have been obscured, even lost, at times, in the history of English teaching in schools. The dungeons of Doubting Castle have then been reoccupied, while successive waves of grammarians, parsing experts, rote-learners, textual hacks, 'back-to-basics' vigilantes, or clinical linguisticians have sought to hold sway over English in the classroom. Yet only an obtuse mind would claim to have some exclusive 'scientific' expertise in the field of language, which is as complex and as variable as human life itself. Continually the key to renewal has been discovered by creative individuals to be within themselves – by provocateurs such as Matthew Arnold, the poet-HMI, who campaigned in the last century for the claims of poetry as a source of both joy and of 'criticism of life' in the school curriculum; by Caldwell Cook, in the early decades of our own century; by George Sampson, whose *English for the English* (1934) is still to be recommended as a classic text on teaching the mother tongue; and by more recent teachers and writers such as James Britton, Marjorie Hourd, David Holbrook, Frank Whitehead, John Dixon, Paddy Creber and Peter Abbs. Yet their kinds of insight have only been realised through the company of teachers who have quietly achieved miracles with their own classes, whether in favourable or unfavourable conditions, without ever bothering to secure themselves even a footnote in a journal or a book. My own English teacher, who wrote no books on English teaching, remains for me still as a civilising influence in my life. A man of learning and wit, he spent much of his teaching life in a modest Midlands city school, where he was content to give of his large store of books and learning, in a continually renewed commitment to his successive generations of pupils. His pupils did not doubt that through his teaching art, he celebrated his living; as with the physician in Dickens' *Little Dorrit*, 'where he was, something real was'. And his presence represented, socially and morally, a dense and serious world, as well as a world of delight in the involvement with literature and drama and the other forms of the imaginative life.

That kind of teaching spirit needs constant renewals and readjustments of method, in the light of the great changes in secondary education of the last two decades, so that the ideal of education for *each*, as well as for *all*, may be achieved. When my own English department launched into mixed ability teaching in a London comprehensive school in the late 'sixties, an initial blind confidence soon gave way to uncertainty, as we took to unfamiliar paths. We found that we could no longer draw so directly on past wisdom, nor even on our own previous (secondary 'grammar' and 'modern') experience. Along with other schools who were taking such directions in a spirit of trust and hope, rather than of firm knowledge and predictions, we had to proceed through trial and much error. At that time it seemed that we had to construct wholly for ourselves the kinds of teaching patterns that were needed; it was only gradually – through meetings often convened by ourselves – that we gained access to the good fruits of work in other schools, to add to our own co-labour. Teachers still have to work too much and too long in isolation from each other; yet looking round now, it can be better seen that there have been many good teachers, advisers and teacher-trainers at work in the field of English studies, who have put the inheritance of the past to good use, when labouring for innovation in the new teaching contexts. It is important that the common strands of such good work – work achieved sometimes in the face of difficulties, incomprehension and even opposition – should be drawn together. Without sustained effort at continuity here, the case for the poetic basis of English might otherwise be curtailed once more, under already quite long-sustained pressures for educational 'cuts'. Like Brocklehurst's passion to shear off Jane Eyre's excessively handsome hair, there is a tendency when cuts are proposed for a certain mean-spirited utilitarianism to grow, especially where the arts in education are concerned.

The uses of fiction, poetry and drama are not obvious to a Brocklehurst (except, as an 'accomplishment' for a privileged élite); therefore, the argument goes at its crudest, let the English department confine itself to so-called 'basics' (of spelling, punctuation, and so on). In this way, the actual proportion of English and drama specialists in our schools becomes threatened; for who needs specialists any longer, if English is 'just a matter of basics'? Yet the experienced specialist knows that a language diet deprived of creative content and activity *has* no true 'basics', and has no chance of generating opportunities to teach the good manners of spelling, punctuation and so on; it would be like teaching table manners without any food on the table. Where the quality of language, of cultural growth is concerned, it is best that we think, in Blake's phrase, of providing 'enough – or excess'. To evade the needs of our children for imaginative experience is to evade the best connections that can be made with the visible and sensible world. In time, it is an evasion that would not be lightly forgiven by those children.

Art-discourse

One difficulty that preoccupies many present-day English teachers is that we now seem to lack any commonly agreed *aesthetic*, any tried and workable theory of what art is and does, which might help to secure an art-presence in English teaching. This is not an easy (or even an obvious) task to have to face. Neither may this book, with its commitment to the practice of teaching, stay long for an answer. But some working notes are needed, in order to show at least the direction in which the answers might lie.

I have suggested elsewhere (1979) how a single work by Robin Collingwood might provide a valuable basis for such an aesthetic. Published over forty years ago now, his *Principles of Art* (1939) establishes Collingwood as a powerful maker of principles, and as an exceptionally sensitive commentator on the arts. In this book he sought to rescue art from the sometimes ancient confusions that it has suffered with other kinds of human action or achievement. Art, he declares, is not to be confused with craft or skill as the Greeks confused it, apparently for all posterity, in their use of the blanket term *teknai* for 'art and craft'. Nor is it to be confused with propaganda, which (like craft) always has premeditated and calculated didactic intentions. Nor yet is it to be confused with entertainment, which operates again from calculated intentions towards a limited aim. Art may contain some elements of all three of these, but essentially it has a unique, not general, character; and it is far more significant in intention and achievement than any of them; for it is devoted to the emerging of meaningful forms of individually lived experience. Art is nothing less than the revealed experience of our own living, our own being. We express and communicate our visions of experience through making the forms of art. And it follows that response to art – when both the art and the response are authentic – is itself a creative, artistic activity, since our responses are in the first place invariably intuitive and feeling-based, generating in turn a more complex ordering of response and interpreting, as we develop towards full encounter with the work of art. The intention and achievement of authentic art is, in short, to reveal the truth – the truth that only the body can affirm. Edgar declares in the wake of Lear's great tragedy that our obligation is to 'speak what we feel, not what we ought to say'. Collingwood offers the insight more prosaically, but the elaboration of his judgement is impressive:

> His business as an artist is to speak out, to make a clean breast. But what he has to utter is not, as the individualistic theory of his art would have us think, his own secrets. As spokesman of his community, the secrets he must utter are theirs. The reason why they need him is that no

community altogether knows its own heart; and by failing in this knowledge a community deceives itself on the one subject concerning which ignorance means death. For the evils which come from that ignorance the poet as prophet suggests no remedy because he has already given one. The remedy is the poem itself. Art is the community's medicine for the worst disease of mind, the corruption of consciousness.

Writing on the eve of the outbreak of the Second World War, Collingwood concluded that it is on art, or the conscious realising of art in our language and culture and living, that our very existence, let alone our 'flowering' may depend. For Collingwood, artistic modes of thought are not a luxury, but an essential means of survival. The main roots of a language are nourished through artistic activity. Art is the revealing of the human quest for truth. And that, let it be added, is the goal of all creative discourse, and of all authentic learning. It is what we are about, at best, in using, teaching and learning language.

It follows, that as teachers of language we should recognise the primary importance for our lives of all the expressive arts – kinetic, visual, musical, literary, verbal. As learners or teachers, we seek then to be continually engaged and re-engaged in art disciplines – especially, of course, in the language arts of literature, drama, art-speech. These are the disciplines through which English studies will flourish, and which offer, at best, a true basis for any genuinely individual expression of experience. To speak of 'discipline' here is not to advance the claims for the kinds of pseudo 'lit.-crit.' games, whether scholarly-ancient or clinical-modern, that literary studies sometimes decline into, when attention and commitment are not of the best; it is to plead rather against all inert versions of textual studies, for the sake of the very life of the language. When D. H. Lawrence declared (in *Studies in Classic American Literature*, 1919) that 'art speech is the only truth'; and when he says through Ursula in *Women in Love*, that 'the word of art is only the truth about the real world, that's all', he is not merely advancing the special claims of some sub-species of language (as distinct from, say, the language of scientific discourse, of gossip in a pub, the language I am using now, and so on). The nature of art-discourse, in any kind of language context, lies in its being an authentic expression of questing thought by you and me, when every word, phrase and pause counts in revealing the witness of the living individual and its impact on the listener and reader. There should always be art-discourse; or (to modify just a little) the roots of art-speech should always be nourishing the discourse of the learner, the teacher, the living human being. It is indeed the teacher's responsibility to allow – and even, when necessary, coerce – the learner to acknowledge and take up full responsibility for and commitment to what he says. But the 'coercing' must be of that rare kind which simply insists on respect for the self-being of the learner, and which is prepared to wait for the learner's self-responsibility to emerge. For the learner's own language is redolent of his/her otherness – it is of his/her body. Discovering the world through touch, vision, hearing, smelling, tasting, and giving shapes to these discoveries in language forms: these are acts of the body, through which personal meanings are offered and shared. The individual's experience comes in turn to affect the public meanings that we hold in common, within our several contexts.

Lawrence's own notions about art-speech are tellingly applied in his criticism; but they are not original, of course, any more than are our own present proposals for the 'poetic' basis of language. The source of such notions goes back at least to the beginnings of the Romantic Movement. It springs specifically from Wordsworth's treatise on poetry and language, in *The Preface* to the *Lyrical Ballads*, a text which has found its way into virtually every important discussion about the language of poetry ever since. In the *Preface*, Wordsworth advances his central point about the nature of poetry – that 'there neither is nor can be any essential difference' between poetry and prose, for they 'both speak by and to the same organs'. And in itself, the *Preface* provides its own evidence as to the nature of art-discourse, whether as prose or poetry. It stands as a heartfelt personal statement about the nature of language and poetry, and is at the same time a classic piece of strenuously argued rational discourse. Reason serves emotion, emotion employs reason, as the writer works sincerely at the effort to say what he means, from what he has felt. The writer is an ordinary man, who is also a poet 'speaking to men'. The difference between the *Preface* and the poetry that follows is, he declares, simply one of degree, rather than of kind. The poetry will be more actual for being rooted in ordinary discourse, in the ordinary transactions of living; while the prose will be the richer for adopting some of the rules of 'selection' of ordinary speech that are operated by the poet. We may take note for ourselves that in this crucial principle of 'selection' from the language of common usage, lie all the possibilities of a refined yet vigorous cultural life. But Wordsworth does not start out with preconceived notions of 'high culture'. Nothing, he declares, is too trivial to be worth poetic regard; for the richest fabric of our lives is composed, and can hardly be otherwise composed, of such ordinary moments and events.

On Wordsworth's trust in the formative powers of the ordinary person, in ordinary contact with daily living, are grounded his beliefs about the nature of the very highest achievement in language, in poetic experience. It is just such a trust in ourselves, and in our children, which ought to underwrite our notions about language as the personal possession of each ordinary individual. From this, it follows that our policies in teaching language will be guided by an intention to work according to the grain of actual needs, desires, yearnings and imaginings in the growing individual. Our ingenuity as teachers will be tested through providing tasks and resources – especially art-resources – for the 'potentially creative space' of the learner (that phrase is Donald Winnicott's, used in his account of playing and learning relationships in *Playing and Reality*, 1971).

Thus entrusted and encouraged, thus engaged and quickened,

learners may then seek to shape their own language patterns, to make sure of their living according to their own variant individuality. For our very being is lodged in our language, as our language is in our being; and only through our language can we declare ourselves to others, to the world, thus validating both ourselves and the world.

Yet how much English teaching and language 'intervention' is genuinely composed of serious play in the spirit of these truths, is a respectful negotiating between teacher and learners of their several experiences – of text, or film, or event, or moral issue? There is still an abundance in primary schools of mechanically 'progressive' reading schemes; in secondary schools, of mechanically 'progressive' course books for English studies; and throughout the age-range, of grammar-punctuation exercises, split off from any personal engagement in living. Such schemes and activities are spiritedly attacked from time to time, in print and in teachers' meetings. But where the criticisms are met at all, they are usually dismissed with varying degrees of ingenuousness, as 'ignoring the needs of the inexperienced/tired/overworked teacher'; or as 'denying the learner's needs for a framework'; or even, as ignoring the need for 'basic' standards. Yet what cannot be rationalised away, is the fact that all such schemes are spawned from a view that work and learning are mere matters of predictable routine, even if (as in the better versions of these schemes) the routine can become mildly enjoyable at times. Such a view of work cannot entertain the notion of serious play as a guiding principle in learning, since it must deny the teacher's and the learner's creative (and therefore essentially unpredictable) engagement in their learning. Granted, the needs of the inexperienced and the overworked teacher ought to be respected. Granted too that there must be some framework for the syllabus, to ensure balance and continuity. And further, granted that the alleged 'basics', or 'decencies' of spelling, punctuation, handwriting, syntax and so on, will need careful attention in a sensibly planned English course. But if we intend to work from real 'basics', we cannot forget one quite basic truth about the acquiring of language: that living language is interwoven with living being. Thus to intervene in, or even simply to encourage language development is potentially to enter private, even secret areas. Respect for the otherness of the learner is of the essence. We find the notion of physical 'cloning' repugnant; why should we then be any more patient with language-learning 'programmes' which assume a right to predict an undeviating path of language development for an individual?

The Informing Body

To draw attention to Wordsworth's sense of himself as an 'ordinary man' is not to deny his rare innovative genius, his place as a major poet. It is, rather, to make a larger claim than is usually acceptable to schools, the media, universities and colleges, for the creative capacity of the 'ordinary' learner. This creative capacity may doubtless become inert among whole communities of people; and just as Wordsworth complained about 'sickly and stupid' novels that both reflected and damaged further the state of sensibility in his own times, we too might be tempted merely to mourn the damage done in our own era by the sorry heaps of bad films, computer-processed songs, soap-box television and prostituted newspapers. Their combined forces seem to remain as impervious to the attacks of modern semiotics-based criticism as they did to the moral protests of a previous generation. Yet the whole impact of the *Preface*, and of the poems that followed, is optimistic. For Wordsworth's (and Coleridge's) vision perceives how our bodies have the power not only to receive signs from one world, but also have the power to transmit to the world, in phenomenological relationship. Through new encounter, we create new meaning. Despite his own professed admiration for Hartley's notions of the mind as a vacant space waiting to be filled with the world's objects, Wordsworth's prose and poetry in the *Lyrical Ballads* attest to the power of the creative individual to *confer* meaning on the world, not merely to receive. (One important implication of this, for example, concerns the possibilities of imaginative involvement with the media in English studies – a point taken up in John Hodgson's chapter on the presenting of film and television in the English lesson.) Nor can Wordsworth's thesis be dismissed as being merely something of the past, and now superseded; for in the light of more recent modern phenomenological thought there is now established a clear philosophical alternative to the Cartesian notion of mind-body split which has dominated Western thought for so long, and which provided the premises of modern logical positivism in the twentieth century. Books such as Maurice Merleau-Ponty's *The Phenomenology of Perception* (1962), together with the contributions of thinkers like Grene and Polanyi, are directed to altering our notions about the nature of truth, and have highlighted in particular (as far as teaching and learning are concerned) the responsibility that each individual necessarily inherits for the quality of truth and knowledge. This is not the place to dwell in detail on philosophical issues; but it is a matter of urgency that our educational-discourse, as well as our attention to principles of English teaching, should now be directed in phenomenological spirit. The influence of the new insights is perhaps only now beginning to affect thinking in education; and interestingly, it was the arch anti-philosopher critic F. R. Leavis himself who eventually drew attention in *The Living Principle* (1975) to the primary importance of such philosophical writings as those of Michael Polanyi and Marjorie Grene, and their importance for English (and educational) studies.

To live from the body's experience, not from abstraction: that is the true quest of the language of learning and teaching. It requires, too, more even than admission of our subjectivity, for it requires us to put our subjectivity to the test; first to reveal what we truly feel, then to defend – and adjust – our vision, through dialogue with others. This disposition to embrace the actual requires a simplicity and a creative courage which is present in all genuine art. Lucidity in art-discourse depends on the distinctness, the singleness of our individual view, achieved through our meetings and actions with others; and not – as it becomes in narrowed-down positivism – through the hoped for production of some kind of universally unambiguous and perfectly 'objective' language, from which subjective insights must be safely excluded. That could only be, and remain, still-born – a language fit for homunculi and robots.

To sum up: the language of learning, at any age, at any level, involves an effort towards meaning, towards truth. It is the most important enterprise in which an individual can engage. Our language has a poetic basis and seeks embodiment in the many forms of expression – spoken, musical, written, painted – of art-discourse. All of us, in so far as we express our lived perceptions, act with artistic intent, since our language is itself an act of endowing, is a creative contributing to human understanding. Meanings are created through language, when the presence of both the subjective self (the speaker) and the presence of the other (the audience) are acknowledged and where there is an individual effort of reaching from one to the other. Expression is realised through communication, thus making our experience real. Georges Gusdorf recognised this in his illuminating book *Speaking* (1965):

> Pure expression, detached from communication, remains a fiction, because all speech implies aiming towards others. True communication is the realization of a unity, i.e. a piece of common labour. I cannot communicate as long as I do not try to bring to the others the profound sense of my being.

Against the Cliché

Clichés reflect habit-bound and worn-out versions of living; you cannot have a fresh, unclichéd language style without a fresh, unclichéd vision of life. Learner and teacher together need their *own* language, and to beware of any reassuring-looking yet rotten planks of jargon and prejudice, thrown together as bridges of authoritative discourse. It is not, of course, easy to be a teacher or learner in this sense. It is easier to deny what we have actually seen or felt, to join the ranks of the compliant. We now quite often use the term 'exist' in a rather unhappy way, as though 'existing' were at a level rather below living, below creative contact with our world – followers, sheep, the easily led, those who merely 'exist'. Yet the roots of the term lie in the Latin verb *ex-sistere*: to stand out, to emerge, to become visible, to become manifest. To live 'existentially' in fact, is to insist on one's own irreducible presence; it is to make stances of resisting as well as of existing. Thus we shall not merely comply with the predictions of economists, behaviourists, political manipulators nor anyone who would claim to reduce to a science the infinite, complex and subtle variables of being human. Propaganda, persuasion, insinuation, abstract assurances shall all be tested thoroughly, in the light of our own real experience of things. Only then shall we discover our own forms of expression and communication, our intention, our own meanings.

In *Man and People* (1957) which sets out to expound the principles of a new sociology, the Spanish phenomenologist Ortega y Gasset reveals how the quality of one's language is inseparable from the quality of one's concern for truth. Ortega writes essentially poetically; he is a master of illuminating metaphor. He is specially drawn to images from the chase; his prose is full of the tautness of the body supply stretched, and of muscles under stress, of the hunter and the quarry, so that his teaching style conveys the strange sense of hair-raisingly urgent occasion, insisting that he and his audience should justify what could at worst be a lost hour expended together. He offers, for instance, a memorable two-word insight to formulate his notion of the learner, the seeker-for-truth, who is prepared to offer full bodily – embracing the psychic and spiritual – commitment to the search. Taking Nietzsche's famously disastrous advice – disastrous to himself, to our century – to 'live dangerously!', Ortega acknowledges what made Nietzsche offer such a command. At all costs, Nietzsche had urged, avoid living conventionally, avoid accepting the life of clichés. But Ortega's neatly contrary solution to the problem is, 'Live alertly!' Be quick and wary in a world full of unexpected danger to our well-being and even our survival – a world already far too dangerous to allow for lunatics who want to live even more dangerously. Paradoxically, we need to find the strength and art to survive through becoming vulnerable; we must risk self-exposure, in order to gain space for our subjectivity. For philosophy is the discipline that would pursue truth through 'criticism of conventional life': it insists that we must be content with our own being when we propose to formulate what we claim to know. Philosophy, he declares:

> . . . is not a science but if you like, an indecency, since it consists in baring things and oneself, stripping them to stark nakedness – to what they are and I am – and that is all. Philosophy is truth, the terrible and desolate, solitary truth of things. Truth means things laid open, and that is the literal meaning of the Greek word for truth – letheia – that is, to lay bare.

We are English teachers, rather than philosophers. But do we wish to be concerned with anything less than the truth? Rather than seeing our task as being the purveying and consuming of so many chunks of language or knowledge, convenience-wrapped for the 'market-place of education', we can join in hunting the elusive living quarry of the thing-to-be-named-and-learned; and in translating that quarry into ourselves, just as early caveman did through the marvellously attentive language of his cave paintings.

To conclude this Introduction, I should re-direct our attention to the classroom; and in particular to the writings of a learner who is engaged with a literary text. It is a piece of writing which meets well what Ortega required of the truth-seekers – that there should be a *self*-confronting in any confronting with the 'other', in order to ensure truthfulness in the encounter. The writing is a passage from an essay by a boy aged sixteen, still in the first term of his lower sixth year in a London comprehensive school. He has been studying two very demanding texts during the term – Shakespeare's *King Lear* and Golding's *Pincher Martin* – and like the rest of the class he has been required to engage in a prolonged, sometimes painful struggle to make sense of the term's work. He was one of a group who were quite familiar with texts of quality – they had read Pinter's plays, Lawrence's short stories, Dickens' *Great Expectations* in their 'mixed ability' fifth year class. But these new texts had raised more daunting, existential issues; and Philip reflects on these, towards the end of a long 'final piece for the term' essay on the two texts:

From *Reflections on two set books*

. . . In both books, *King Lear* and *Pincher Martin*, that we are reading at present there is a great deal of searching for identities and to a great extent this is like the world today because at one time or another each of us searches for some kind of identity to relate to.

Pincher Martin himself, is perhaps the best example of someone searching for their identity but, within himself, he knows that he has left it too late and his constant struggling throughout the book emphasises this point. He is so scared and unsure of himself that he has to struggle – his life has been a struggle so he mustn't give up his struggling – it is his only hope for survival. Pincher has never before thought in search of his identity. For all he cared there wasn't an identity for him to search for. He was just a number in the Navy and that is all he identified with. He had never thought that there was a reason for his life and that there was an identity to seek but when he was left, stranded in the sea this hidden search for his identity overpowered him and he was made to fend for himself. Never before had he been alone as he was now and because he didn't really know what he was capable of he had to try and search for his identity. Perhaps the only real truth that Pincher obtained from life was from those last dying moments. It was during this time that he realised he was a nobody and his true identity could never really have been found in the navy – his life hadn't meant anything and it had been wasted.

Pincher hadn't really achieved anything from life – he had been subconsciously dead to himself throughout his life. The achievements he had reckoned with had been things like promotion and exam-passes. Spiritual and emotional achievements had never come into the reckoning for he had never tried to gain them and hence had never succeeded in doing so. My theory is that life is a kind of jig-saw puzzle and every now and again you strive to gain more, not necessarily material but mental, each piece of the jig-saw is gradually put in it's allotted place. A useful unwasted and satisfying life may have the whole picture full with all the pieces placed, but some lives or pictures may be very empty and hardly any of the pieces will have been used.

The latter jig-saw puzzle will be something like Pincher's life for he has hardly gained anything from life and there are a great many segments of his life that still need to be filled in. The only pieces of the jig-saw that will have been filled in are those that Pincher struggled to secure at the end of his life at those last dying struggling moments.

I know for certain that I won't be a 'Pincher Man' when I die for even though, I hope, I have many years to come, I am sure I know more about myself than Pincher ever would have known. In fact, although it may sound deceitful, even though I am very quiet, a lot of this term has been spent thinking of myself and the way life is going and in fact many a time I have been near breaking point. I'm sure I would have passed this point by now if I hadn't carefully scanned the situation and then realised I had got a reason for life and a true identity to reach. I haven't found this identity yet, in fact I am going through a very confused and searching phase recently where I have been unusually tense and withdrawn but I find that writing and expressing myself on paper has helped a lot and breaks down these barriers that are holding me very easily. Perhaps Pincher would have found more about himself had he attempted, but he didn't and hence the cold, harsh, un-real way in which he died symbolised the way he had lived and been driven into the cause of the way he died.

King Lear could also be likened to Pincher in that he never finds his true identity also. Lear, on the other hand, has heroically tried to do so though, although succeed he does not. During the book I find Lear to be a very restless, searching and confused man. I somehow feel that life doesn't come up to Lear's great expectations. Being a King, he feels that his life should be full of happiness but he doesn't want to make his happiness for himself. I agree that happiness should hold a great deal of our lives but I feel we must experience woe for us to feel so much for happiness. These emotions, good or bad, make up our lives and we must learn to take the rough with the smooth. Lear just won't face this and that is why he is so confused when his daughters turn against him. Lear's world is based greatly on material things – he thinks he can buy his daughter's love and respect for him by giving them parts of his Kingdom but he has 'bought' their respect once too often and they pay him back for his foolishness by going against him. Lear should also have realised that material gains aren't the only things in life for there are also the spiritual gains which Lear only realises when it is far too late . . .

My restlessness has been nearly banished although Pincher's never was. All I hope is that by the time my life expires I will have a satisfying outlook on life; I know we all go through certain phases in our lives when the reason for living or search for identity might not look so bright but if that far reaching glimmer of light at the end of our dark tunnel is still flickering there then we know that life is worth living.

In terms of formal 'Advanced level standards' this passage is open to various criticisms: it lacks critical perspective, in seeming to value *Pincher Martin* as highly as *King Lear*; it offers no detailed attention to the text (though this had been given earlier in the essay); it is strongly personal, and there are some errors of phrasing, and so on. But there is a kind of achievement here which is still rare in 'A' level English Literature writing, in that Philip has taken genuine personal risks in reflecting on these texts. They have taken him down a seeming 'dark tunnel' of doubt and fear, and he has been involved in a far more important effort towards understanding and meaning, than merely just preparing for the immediate hurdles of 'A' levels and University. His personal effort reveals the very essence of the artistic/critical spirit; from this we may trust that the known techniques and modes of criticism will be properly adopted, not just employed in the too familiar and meaningless rituals of 'lit.-crit.' that can come to replace genuine – that is, personal – engagement with the text. Philip has successfully related creative art, as represented in these texts, to his own discourse, his own living.

References

1 Books on English Teaching

ABBS, P. (1979) *Reclamations* (Heinemann)
COOK, H. CALDWELL (1915) *Perse Playbook No. 4* (Cambridge University Press)
CREBER, J. W. P. (1982) *Sense and Sensitivity* (Revised Edition) (School of Education, University of Exeter)
DIXON, J. (1975) *Growth through English* (Revised Edition) (Oxford University Press)
HOLBROOK, D. (1979) *English for Meaning* (NFER)
HOURD, M. (1959) *The Education of the Poetic Spirit* (Heinemann)
JACKSON, D. (1982) *Continuity in Secondary English* (Methuen)
MATHIESON, M. (1975) *The Preachers of Culture* (Allen and Unwin)
SAMPSON, G. (1934) *English for the English* (Cambridge University Press)
STRATTA, L., DIXON, J. and WILKINSON, A. M. (1973) *Patterns of Language* (Heinemann)
WHITEHEAD, F. S. (1966) *The Disappearing Dais* (Chatto)

2 Others

BARNES, D. (1976) *From Communication to Curriculum* (Penguin)
BRITTON, J. (1970) *Language and Learning* (Penguin)
CALOUSTE GULBENKIAN FOUNDATION (1982) *The Arts in Schools: Principles, Practice and Provision*
COLLINGWOOD, R. (1939) *Principles of Art* (Oxford University Press)
GUSDORF, G. (1965) *Speaking (La Parole)* (Northwestern University Press)
HARRISON, B. T. (1979) *Poetry and the Language of Feeling* (Tract No. 27, Gryphon Press)
HARRISON, B. T. (1983) *Learning through Writing* (NFER/Nelson)
HOURD, M. (1972) *Relationship in Learning* (Heinemann)
LEAVIS, F. R. (1975) *The Living Principle* (Cambridge University Press)
MACMURRAY, J. (1962) *Emotion and Reason* (Revised Edition) (Faber)
MERLEAU-PONTY, M. (1962) *The Phenomenology of Perception* (Routledge and Kegan Paul)
ORTEGA Y GASSET, J. (1957) *Man and People* (Allen and Unwin)
WILKINSON, A. M. (1975) *Language and Education* (Oxford University Press)
WINNICOTT, D. W. (1971) *Playing and Reality* (Tavistock)
WORDSWORTH, W. (1798) *Preface* to the *Lyrical Ballads* (Reprinted)

1 Speaking and Listening: Coming to Know

Peter Clough

For most of the last fifty years, and up to the appearance of Wilkinson's *Spoken English* (1965), if it was thought about much at all, then classroom speaking was seen largely as a discrete skill to be developed towards particular ends like play-acting or public speaking or debate. At best, pupils might have been asked to prepare a two-minute talk; or plays were read around the class with the same articulate few getting the main parts. Apart from this limited role, children's talk in the classroom was discouraged. Usually the role assigned to them was that of passive listener, while talking was done by the teacher as a sort of rhetoric; information had to be transmitted persuasively, though more often it was done indifferently.

Am I being hard on the men and women who taught me? Has my own performance in the classroom improved on theirs? A sort of pseudo-science has been brought lately to the study of language in education, which might lead us to think that practice has actually changed. But the question remains as to whether we have merely elaborated our principles and left the dais largely undisturbed. Educationists have described the shift from the curriculum to the child, from an approach which emphasised skills to one which gives status to personal experience. The move is from behavioural to 'inner' processes, and we have come to see speech and language generally as not only revealing of this 'life within' but as the very means by which this life is possible, by which it is enriched, and by which it becomes more properly an 'outer', a shared life. We are becoming persuaded that we can teach ourselves the meaning of our thought as we try to make it explicit for others. One of Douglas Barnes' achievements is to have alerted teachers to the importance of letting children speak and *think* through speaking. In this chapter, I want to describe something of what happens when children speak; then I want to emphasise that listening is an art which teachers must develop if they are to appreciate and build on this talk.

Language Accomplishes Thought

We can never really know how much learning takes place at a tacit level which may not be called upon for explanation. We certainly know much more than we can ever explain, and our language may serve to articulate some of this knowledge. It has been said that language accomplishes thought, and I think what is meant by this may be illustrated by the following example. Kevin is one of a group of four Sixth Formers of 'average' achievement in a large urban comprehensive. Though unused to working like this, the group had been left alone with a tape recorder and asked to discuss Sylvia Plath's poem 'Berck-Plage' from the collection *Ariel*. I quote Kevin from the point at which one of his observations – about the function of the sea in the poem – has just been challenged. He goes on to make a case for his comment, a 'case' which he was clearly unaware of *as such* before this need arose. Transcription reveals how the speech is disjointed and tentative, as is characteristic of exploratory language:

> If you go back to Section 1 then that black cassock, association, it refers to death, doesn't it . . . that's that's a sort of negative thought er and then you get mackerel gatherers she she seems to be alternating in ea ea within each sort of section with positive and negative thoughts and also er just ideas and images and also actual, experiences like probably she's obviously been to this place, she has been to Berck-Plage, erm, and she sees these mackerel gatherers, that sort of shows a positive side of life er and then ideas contrast er between death and disease and er the sort of the land and the sea where these people are, I think they, I definitely think that they, that the sea's sort of seen as a, a sort of harbour of life . . .

I think the effect of Kevin's exploration is poetic, in the sense that he finally comes to recreate with some care the experience of the poet. We can conclude that more speaking can mean greater thought, if the circumstances require the sort of speech which is thoughtful.

Yet much of daily speech is an effortless (and apparently thoughtless) sort of maintenance work which seems to exist just to keep things going rather than to innovate thought; the extreme forms of this are clichés, sedimentations of thought which are substitutes for thinking. We should not be so naïve as to think or even hope that our pupils will think and speak in an exciting way all the time; for the most part the maintenance work serves the function of basic communication. But communication is only one pole of language; the other is expression, and it is this which we usually identify as our chief concern as teachers of English.

Expression and Communication

It is not enough to say that communication and expression are always present to speech; the one simply cannot exist without the other. Language must communicate in order to *be* language, and it is the expressive element which reveals the being of the speaker. Expression, then, is to be understood as the personal voice of a writer or speaker giving a description of experience which is at once uniquely his and yet, by virtue of the fact that it is manifestly communicated, must touch and share the experience of the audience. Now it is generally felt that English teaching nurtures expression, but examples like the following show how it is easy for teachers to obliterate the felt responses of their pupils, in the interest of an explicit communication. Julia, a thirteen-year-old West Indian, is telling a second year remedial class about an experience in the snow after the teacher has given an exposition on the theme of excitement:

> JULIA: We was sliding er sliding right fast and going like anything and so, and so fast that we was falling off and went like anything at the bottom . . . we just laughed and laughed.
>
> TEACHER: How would you describe your feelings I mean at the bottom? (*silence*)
>
> TEACHER: Would you say you were exhilarated for example? Mmm?
>
> JULIA: Yes.

The drive of our education is towards externalising consciousness, towards a disembodied knowledge and a rationality independent of the child. Children are brought to exemplars of knowledge which they must internalise, and their own contributions are seldom respected. In the science subjects, they may be made to feel that their ideas are irrelevant if not worthless before the grand truths of established 'knowledge'. In arts teaching the situation is generally believed to be better; arts teachers asked to identify their aims will normally talk of the development of individuality and self-expression. But the ideal outruns the practice; teachers of English, for example, themselves graduates within a particular form, still seek and reward perfected realisations of that form. They are tempted to praise 'critic-talk' – as distinct from the concern for personally realised truth that is implicit in true criticism – so that a personal and feeling response may be dismissed as badly-expressed, or not objectified or gauche. And although apparently inviting of the felt response it is in fact the 'objectified', received version they really require. Witkin (1974) characterised the teacher who directs the pupils' responses into 'an objective framework that defuses them, as it were'. He found few English teachers who were 'particularly keen to handle the "live" wire of emotion' in their lessons. If we insist on highly stylised language, or if we tactlessly inhibit felt responses which are not yet expressed according to the models we have come to see as exemplary, we shall overlook the value of language which may be on the point of teasing out and enhancing understanding. Allowing and encouraging children to speak obviously fosters communication skills. But it further requires them to give a personal account of themselves which they may not ordinarily be called upon to do; it requires them, that is, to express what they know and what they are coming to know.

Questions and Answers: Who's in Charge Here?

It has been suggested that teachers directly control the sort and quality of this knowing. One obvious way in which they do this is by having a virtual monopoly on the asking of key questions. Children certainly ask questions, but these are most often of a clerical nature (Which page . . ? Where is . . ?) or about vocabulary. Most of the time they are not required to pose searching questions which call for reflection; these questions are part of the way in which the teacher can direct the enquiry to her idea of its ends. In the following transcription the group quoted earlier is looking at another Sylvia Plath poem, but this time it is introduced by the teacher. She has a very clear idea of what she wants to elicit from the poem and from the students, and her questions are efficiently directed towards filling in this preconceived picture of hers:

TEACHER: Why does she call it *The Moon and The Yew Tree?* What's, what's the significance for her? What do you know about yew trees? What do you know about Sylvia Plath and her, erm, identity with the moon?

PUPIL 1: There's some yew trees near her house, isn't there?

TEACHER: That's right, I think it's the house in Devon, isn't it which borders onto the graveyard, and . . . well, what do you know about yew trees, d'you know anything about them?

PUPIL 2: Associated with death, aren't they?

TEACHER: Yeh a-apparently they're usually planted in . . . graveyards, and you do yes usually associate them, not necessarily with death I think but certainly with sorrow. What about the idea of the moon? What's the moon in this poem? How does she see the moon?
(*pause*)

PUPIL 1: She says it's her mother.

TEACHER: It's her mother right, yeh, that's an important thing I think to focus on . . . erm, right shall we start from the beginning . . .

This is good teaching. But there is a sense in which the actual putting of questions can be as important as the finding of answers. Most simply this is because putting questions requires seeing and framing problems. Merely answering someone else's question may amount to a mechanical slot-filling exercise, where the necessity of those answers is not seen as a function of an important question, but rather as a requirement of an externally imposed task. Asking children to spot the areas of difficulty – the areas of *their* difficulty moreover – and to frame *their own* questions is asking them to share in the location of problems. Still with Sylvia Plath and the Sixth Form, the following transcription shows an interpretation of 'Berck-Plage' by a different group from the previous one. Again left by themselves with a tape recorder, they appear to ask questions commensurate with their needs and the pace of the discussion rather than with the critical and strategic considerations of a teacher. Questions occurring like this are experienced as genuine enquiries rather than challenges, and they prompt the sharing of ideas rather than the closing down on one definitive response. The particular lines they are looking at are:

' . . . the mackerel gatherers
Who wall up their backs against him.
They are handling the black and green lozenges like the parts of a
    body.'

Gillian asks:

PUPIL 1:	Why are t'mackerel gatherers walling up their backs against him?
PUPIL 2:	We think that well I think anyway, that mackerel gatherers fishermen they just turn their backs to these people, they don't want to have nothing to do with them, y'know they just turn away from them.
PUPIL 3:	'N that about, lozenges.
PUPIL 2:	Well they're t'fish.
PUPIL 4:	They're t'fish.
PUPIL 1:	And if you notice though, lozenges comes into it a lot and er throughout poem.
PUPIL 5:	And she describes coffin, I mean lozenge, shape of coffin.
PUPIL 2:	Yeh and I think its some reference to t'drugs and pills medication they're on all t'way through.

There are several reasons why such a casual but fruitful exchange is
unlikely to have taken place with the teacher present. Obviously the
pupils view the teacher as an expert and one whose questions are
somewhat artificial in that she knows the answer to them; again, there's
an assumption that there's only one answer. A distinction is often made
between 'closed' questions, which require just one specific response,
and 'open' questions which invite individual reflection and expect a
varied response. The closed question usually has the authority of the
teacher; had a teacher put Gillian's question, I think the response would
have been very different. As it is, it is the same question which might
have the same 'answer' – but it serves here to prompt an open
consideration.

Of course there is no absolute reason why class discussion should not
encourage such openness, but the fact is that it most often fails to. To be
sure it allows for a public airing of ideas, but this public nature makes
very particular demands of language. The opportunity for exploratory
talk is minimal, since children are for obvious reasons not disposed to
venture half-baked ideas in un-planned phrases; Barnes has described
the language of such class discussion as tending to be 'pre-planned' and
'final draft'. At the centre of the discussion is almost invariably the
teacher – who actually needs less language-practice than anybody –
who controls the flow and quality of ideas. He it is who normally draws
the discussion to a close with his characterisation of what has
happened. But the worst feature of teacher-dominated class discussion
is that few children really speak; the opportunity for participation
diminishes not only as the size of the class increases, but also
paradoxically as discussion becomes 'lively' – which is often to say that a
small handful of the more articulate or vociferous or abrasive dominates
the class.

' . . . The Criss-cross of Utterance Between Us'

In asking 'Who's in charge?' I may have implied that it is either the teacher or the group, or one of the group. What has not been considered so far is that the ultimate authority may rest with the material being addressed. In the case of the poetry discussions quoted above, there is no doubt that it is 'in' these texts that the 'answers' lie, though they require mining by discussion and probably the expertise of a teacher (who after all is paid to provide just that). But the majority of English work in schools is not Sixth Form literature; does the observation still hold? I think the next example of group discussion is a valuable reminder that 'meaning' is itself a fuzzy area between the 'facts' which are hung about a text or other work of art, and the experience which an audience brings to that work: talking may be one of the ways to cross this middle ground. This was a bad lesson by any standards, when too busy to attend to them properly, I gave a group of six lively ESN(M) fourteen-year-olds Vaughan Williams' *Fantasia on a Theme by Thomas Tallis* to listen to. The discussion as a whole was not much longer than what is reproduced here, the children having little to say and no guidance. (Only four children speak).

A: I don't myself like it but I can see that its good like.

B: Why's it good if . . .

C: Why's it yeh why . . .

A: Oh I don't have to like it if its I mean for its to be good y'know its I don't know violins and its good.

D: He means its a sort of music I mean a particular and its not what he likes but it has er qualities.

A: Don't tell me what I mean.
(laughter)
(long pause)

D: Music doesn't have to mean anything does it I mean like . . .

B: A poem does like a poem does.

D: Like a poem like a poem like a painting.

B: Oh it does its all this is Arabian nights its all swirly.

D: (Mr) Bradley used to play records at at our Juniors didn't he and he'd and we'd and he'd say now write what you've seen now write what if you felt this 'n if you felt that.

The meaning, the *value* of this exchange is of the same order as that of the music they were listening to – it is in the playing, the speaking, the *event*. This is why language analysis schedules are finally unsatisfactory, because they attribute meanings to the outer shape of words (the sounds or the printed letters) and know nothing of the sculptor of meaning who is working inside those words.

Being more practical, it remains that words are most of what we can know of other people's thought. As teachers committed to some particular *content* in a lesson, there are certain words and phrases we are cued to hear and certain forms of behaviour we read as indicating learning; we may overlook the *process* by which meaning is emerging. It might lie, as in this next example, embedded in desultory chat. Twelve-year-olds, Sean and Mick, are working through some comprehension questions, unaware that they are being recorded. It is in fact the recording and transcription which show up the value of their talk; the teacher was unaware of this and, immediately after this exchange, separated and silenced the boys:

MICK: What's it say then 'is there . . .'

SEAN: 'Is there a reason for Poll's anger?'

MICK: S'obvious obvious. What's next, 'Why does Poll decide not to go to Lowestoft?'

SEAN: Our Eric worked in Lowestoft he worked there.

MICK: 'Why does Poll decide not to go to Lowestoft?' too far for one thing I mean not enough time.

SEAN: Buses Eric went on a bus oh buses yes.

MICK: They didn't have buses then or not buses anyway it doesn't say he decided it doesn't say he decided where is it.

(*pause*)   'Poll looked at the picture and knew he would not go to Lowestoft.'

SEAN: Because he had to be up for work for work in the morning.

MICK: Right shall I put that?

SEAN: Yes no he used that to sort of as a sort of excuse himself see to give himself an excuse.

MICK: He didn't want to go like but he hid that he told himself he hadn't time like.

SEAN: That's good write it.

MICK: You I wrote last one why's Pill sitting with Williams Pill Pill why you sitting with Willy?

PILL: Sir put me.

MICK: Pilly and Willy Right how we going to put this one

Put-put

(*writing*)

'Poll didn't so much decide not to go. It was . . .'

SEAN: Inevitable.

MICK: Inevitable. Pill what you put for number 3 no 4?

PILL: 'Poll decided not to go because it was too late!'

MICK: Typical.

SEAN: That's typical.

MICK: Pill-Poll.

One of the reasons why group talk is not very popular is that for all the time it takes, little ground may in fact be covered. It is particularly as public exams approach that English teachers desert the experience-base and necessarily go for getting some facts across. Whilst exams are with us in their present form we need to be aware of this tension. The other problem is that, where exploration of a text is concerned, pupils may come up with 'wrong' interpretations.

When we accept that one thing grasped personally, if imperfectly, may have more value than many soaked-up as truths from the mouth of the teacher, then we may be satisfied with a more piecemeal progress.

And 'wrong' interpretations may be seen as imperfect realisations of the 'correct', on their way to what's required by a text but arrested at a personal level. 'New' understanding always rests on pre-existing forms of knowledge and of experience. There is obviously no blank space which is filled by a new fact; rather learning requires a reorganising of previous knowing in the light of fresh experience. Now so much teaching seems to want to short-circuit this process and simply to impose on the child some information foreign to his experience. This is not to say that children must have actual and practical experience of every piece of information which the teacher wishes to give them, but that they must be given sufficient opportunity to make the linguistic passage from experience to knowing. Lessons may have a shape and internal consistency at the cost of the pupils' understanding. A teacher identifies his aim and conceives his lesson as a route to that end; his commitment to his projected material and to its presentation in a particular sequence may be the very reason for an inability to start from where the children are. So his responses to what children say are often evaluations of what is in effect a threat to his scheme; they are aberrations or, at best, immature realisations of the teacher's own knowledge, and to be discarded. The language which children use and the thought it represents may be deemed inappropriate to 'school knowledge.' Wilkinson (1971) has said that children are given the jewel of language, but that many are playing marbles with it in the backyard; is it not rather the case that our preoccupation with brilliance blinds us to the elegance and necessity and value of the humbler game? Children's ideas may appear to interpose irrelevantly if viewed from the vantage of the teacher; but what is real to the child cannot be invalidated by mere authority.

Practically, I realise that it cannot be so neatly, so easily, done. The lesson flows, more ground is covered, there is less opportunity for boredom if the teacher remains firmly in control of the speech 'channels', and in any event it is actually impossible to hear what everyone has to say, and to give each pupil a chance to develop his ideas. This is obviously why group methods are so valuable. But even at the level of teacher-led classwork, some of the superficial efficiency must be sacrificed to the more painstaking if less elegant process of bringing about knowledge more certainly.

Learning to Listen

There is talk in the classroom which is 'innocent': it is a routine and daily transactional matter which includes chat and gossip, the maintenance of order, the asking and answering of questions, and so on. Then there is talk which is engineered, in the sense that the teacher intends that speaking shall be an activity as such. We tend to minimise the innocent talk, and to contrive the more artificial version. What is needed is somehow to make classrooms generally noisier places by really following up this insight that speech is heuristic, and essential to the act of learning.

The first methodological principle should be a willingness to negotiate meaning. The example of textual exploration can actually serve as the model of this process; ideas no less than words have variable meanings according to their context and to our perspective. When we wrestle with the meaning of a poem we try its values against our own until we have an understanding which relates both to the 'objective' ideas of the poem and the 'subjective' truth of our experience. The group discussion (whatever its subject) represents this process made public; meanings are arrived at by sharing.

The second principle is that we should be prepared to spend as much time on children's ideas as on those we are trying to teach, because children's experience is the *only* passage by which this material can be realised. This means allowing those awkward gaps in class where thought is apparently slow in coming, and where it would be more expedient to interfere and urge it on where it may not be going, or simply to pass to someone else.

These principles do not mean that we have to affirm every response, force everyone to speak, embarrass individuals and frustrate the class, but that we should be aware of how slowly and *specially* meanings are made. We may need to resist the temptation to recode children's comments in the form of 'What you mean is . . .' statements, and need to avoid a critical terminology which might well stifle an exploratory voice.

Of course this is idealised, optimistic and very time consuming; but children's speech is actually one of the most accessible grounds for really effective research that all teachers have before and around them always – instances of thought which represent so many different views of reality and which call for our understanding and the modification of our practice. A truly arts-centred curriculum must attend to the class as a responding audience; this means training ourselves really to hear what children are saying and thinking. Unfortunately speech is such an autonomous and innocent process that we take it for granted; we assume that we know its meaning simply and, after all, we consider our own speech as teachers to be more important than that of our pupils. The net result is that we are not really sensitive to what is said to us.

Much emphasis has been laid on the importance of the process of exploratory talk. It is seen as providing the opportunity both for expression and for working out ideas which might otherwise remain tacit or unrealised. But we run the risk of elevating the process and minimising the product if we do not pay careful attention to the content of speech. This is to say that group work needs monitoring if the insights articulated by exploratory talk are to be developed and acted upon by the teacher. There needs to be constant play and reference between the more firm knowledge of the teacher and the nascent knowledge of pupils. Letting children talk allows them to accomplish thought; listening to talk allows us to see something of the meaning and value of the thought, and to improve our practice in the light of those meanings.

But it is when children are in fact talking so much less that the teacher needs to be more attentive to the values of what is said. We should not distinguish too keenly between the informal, 'exploratory' talk of the small group and the more formal 'public' statement hazarded by the individual in class. Because these last utterances have to be more finished, more explicit, the teacher tends to see them as more or less firmly held beliefs and hence to bring criteria of rightness and wrongness to them which would not happen with the criss-cross urgency or casualness of group language. An arts-based approach to English teaching must see discourse as something of a work of art *in itself* ('art-speech', it has been called); and, as with any other piece of art, it thrives on how its values are revealed, and is not to be ticked 'right' or dismissed as 'wrong'. We have said that teachers very often hear only what they want or are set to hear; as part of the same function, they may overlook the value of the ideas that are in fact being presented because they are looking and listening for one 'correct' answer, and cannot find relevant or useful an apparently 'wrong' response.

Sorting Out Values and Strategies

These thoughts are a corrective to an extreme 'transmission' version of teaching (to use Barnes' term) which is probably no longer to be found in many schools. But that historical extreme has left a print which will be visible as long as the teacher remains at the centre of class activities, inevitably dispensing meanings rather than negotiating them or listening for alternatives. What remains to be done here is to try and find a practical middle ground between the luxury and idealism of my proposals, and the reality and necessities of work in a classroom. My concluding suggestions will be familiar in the practice of many teachers and are not novel; they aim simply to clarify the values which lie behind these strategies.

Aims and tasks

The 'discussion' lesson cannot be placed in isolation from other work-in-progress. Talk should arise as part of a lesson. Both teacher and pupils need to know why discussion has been organised in a particular way. For the teacher, this will generally be because he wants to ensure that each child has the opportunity for detailed exploration not open to him in the class forum. The pupils, on the other hand, need to have the tasks well-defined, and the criteria by which their efforts will be assessed made explicit. Once sure of his aims, the teacher's arrangements for grouping suggest themselves.

Groups large and small

Pair work is undoubtedly useful, since it is such a natural grouping.

Children do just spontaneously turn to their neighbour to discuss things. The teacher can choose to bring this about more formally at any time by breaking off or into class activities and inviting consideration of ideas in pairs. After a few minutes the class activity can resume and those views be shared. With small groups (say, three to six pupils) it is easier to have fairly stable groups composed of children who sit next or near to each other, so that there is no noisy logistical problem. In principle the teacher should be able to announce group work and have them talking within minutes. Having the same children always talking together in this way has the disadvantage that they come to know and anticipate each other's views and styles, and discourse runs the risk of being short-circuited by intimacy. On the other hand there is a lot to be gained from children's familiarity with each other's ideas and personalities, and constant *ad hoc* grouping means they cannot build up a mutually supportive group approach. There really are no hard and fast rules, and groups should be adjusted according to how they appear to perform. The particularly garrulous and timid need special attention and judicious placing.

There may still be a place for the class discussion, but I have yet to see one which could *truly* be called this, and which is more than the teacher trying rather vainly to defy what seems to be a natural law, that in any large group only a few can really participate.

Expertise: pupils and teacher

Although we seem to talk effortlessly, speaking to some purpose does require effort, and children do need some guidance (and goading) if they are really to learn how to use these opportunities to learn by speaking. Learning to learn takes time, and group work is in many ways much harder work for the teacher than the traditional class lesson or teacher-dominated discussion, though potentially more rewarding. The value of the small group approach lies in the *process* of confrontation between pupil and text, or subject; the end product may in fact be the result of the teacher's final shaping. This will be necessary according to the expertise of the children concerned. It is undoubtedly hard and noisy work for the teacher who needs to learn when and how to intervene, and how indeed to assess what is happening around him. It may be some time before he is convinced that he is not merely licensing chat. (It may be even longer before his headteacher is persuaded!)

Monitoring

Tape recorders are a mixed blessing. They certainly allow teachers to play back what has happened out of his hearing, and they thus impose some requirement to get on with the work on the children; but they can induce tape-consciousness and self-consciousness. I think if we can answer the question, 'Why use tape recorders?' for ourselves, then judicious practice will follow. Remember, though, that five or six groups in one room can defy even the most sensitive machines to record anything decipherable.

However, we can help sensitise ourselves to the meanings of speech by listening regularly to other teachers' lessons, and by recording many different instances of children talking in pairs, in groups, in class, informally as well as formally and then studying these events. It is certainly not necessary to be familiar with the standard techniques for interpreting and categorising language, since the teacher's own intuitive response is likely to be more useful because he/she actually knows the children involved. Arresting and examining speech in any way may be artificial; but there is no doubt that it can teach us something of the hidden values that are lost in the innocence or rapid everyday language; Sean and Mick's teacher was genuinely alarmed to discover that so much desirable activity had been going on without his knowing.

A final example

You have introduced the class to a poem, which has been read aloud a couple of times and some general prefatory remarks have been shared. The class divides into groups and one pupil in each group is asked to act as a sort of chairman, 'in charge' not of the discussion but of keeping it relevant to tasks which you have specified; this pupil will also note and report any conclusions the group comes to. Each group is given a set of questions, which in the early days need to be fairly specific, for they are the substitute for the authority of the teacher and necessary to the motivation and confidence of the group. (Later they can become introductory guide-lines, optional spring-boards for discussion. Later still, a group might be expected to identify its own problems and to formulate the questions it would like answered.) In a sense the teacher's work really begins here as he/she travels the class listening, really *listening* not so much for the signs of explicit activity as for the silences which need some gentle piercing and those which will resolve themselves. At some point after five or fifteen minutes according to how things seem to be going, the class meets again, and the chairman reports on the group's efforts. It remains the teacher's task to draw things together, to ensure that all groups are heard and to offer some conclusions. In the case of literary exploration, and particularly for exam work, it may be essential for the teacher to ensure that the class settles on an 'acceptable' interpretation.

This chapter dwells on the basic principles of developing a particular attitude to speaking. It asks us to see speech not only as a fundamental way of learning, but to see it as the most patent way we have of declaring and negotiating our values. This is equally true for the very young, for the potential scholar, for the disaffected – for all, indeed, who speak to live. Such theoretical issues are primarily important because if we are sure what our aims and principles are, and of what we really mean when we say our concern is 'expression', then good practice should naturally, if not always easily, follow. For my part I feel I am still struggling with these basic questions, and although my own practice improves only haltingly, I am convinced and excited by the evidence of children coming to know which I can see but most importantly hear.

References and Bibliography

BARNES, D. and SCHEMILT, D. (1974) 'Transmission and Interpretation' in *Educational review*, 26:3:213

BARNES, D. (1976) *From Communication to Curriculum* (Penguin)

GUSDORF, G. (1965) *Speaking (La Parole)* (Northwestern University Press)

HOLBROOK, D. (1979) *English for Meaning* (NFER)

PLATH, S. (1965) *Ariel* (Faber)

STUART, S. (1969) *Say!* (Nelson)

TORBE, M. and PROTHEROUGH, R. (1976) *Classroom Encounters* (Ward Lock Educational)

WILKINSON, A. (1965) *Spoken English* (University of Birmingham)

WILKINSON, A. (1971) *The Foundations of Language* (Oxford University Press)

WITKIN, R. (1974) *The Intelligence of Feeling* (Heinemann)

This is not a select bibliography and so I cite three very different books which have less to do with the nuts and bolts than with the ideas behind this chapter. Holbrook's work is always exciting, and *English for Meaning* is central to our concerns with expression; Stuart's *Say!* relates English teaching to Freudian psychology, and is an account of a real engagement with language in the classroom; the Gusdorf book gives a clear and succinct phenomenology of language.

2 Art-response in Reading and Writing

Peter Abbs

And to speak a little metaphysically, words are not a mere vehicle, but they are powers either to kill or animate.

Wordsworth to W. R. Hamilton, 23 December 1829

In this chapter I shall argue that both reading and writing are expressive activities. They require the most subtle acts of imaginative participation and emotional fidelity. As it is my conviction that the key to promoting the teaching of these disciplines in the classroom is to first powerfully develop them in the teacher I shall dwell on my work with Postgraduate Certificate in Education (PGCE) students and teachers on in-service courses. For me it is axiomatic that the teacher has experienced what he seeks to engender in the classroom. Without self-consciousness or insistence, the teacher himself has to become a living exemplar of what it is to be creative. Yet while my emphasis and many of my examples derive from work with student-teachers, I hope that the implications for daily classroom practice as well as for the general running of a coherent English Department, with its centre firmly in the Arts, will become clear. I shall begin by describing the broad problems facing the teaching of reading and writing of literature (and, particularly, of poetry because it is the prototypical form of all imaginative literature) and then continue by trying to establish a reciprocal conversation between guiding theoretical principle and good classroom practice.

Every year students who join the University of Sussex PGCE course are asked to write, before the academic year begins, an autobiographical reflection on their previous educational experience. These often highly personal and perceptive accounts of schools and teachers, of texts and subjects, are not evaluated but read by the tutors, before forming the opening section of the journal which the students will then be expected to keep for the whole year, to chart and reflect upon their own development. It is not easy to summarise their diverse content, but, nevertheless, there is a fairly common pattern which I have come to detect over the years. It is a pattern in which the experience of school from primary school onwards is seen not as a progressive deepening and extending of consciousness, but rather as a systematic narrowing down, a relentless drawing in of the mind to concentrate its attention on the fixed facts and stereotyped remnants of emotion demanded by the Examination Industry, from 'O' level to Degree level. The reading of these autobiographies (though, of course, by no means all fit this pattern) would be dispiriting but for the fact that the very negativity creates its opposite in the student's aspirations: because learning has often been such a sterile experience, the student-teacher now earnestly wishes to create in the classroom an engaged and open encounter.

The following extracts from an autobiographical account by Melanie Porter characterise the kind of reflection I have been describing. As her account is so detailed, and as it relates to the place of reading and writing in English studies – the central theme of my chapter – I shall quote it at some length. Her reflections take us directly and unapologetically into the heart of our theme:

> When I was about ten I had an English teacher who encouraged me to write stories or poems and also to illustrate them. The whole emphasis was on enjoyment and drifting off where you wanted, it was too good an opportunity to miss. I have just been looking at my old school books, which I kept because I am a hoarder rather than for any other reason, but for once they proved useful. They are full of mistakes but also contain an astonishing enthusiasm that I had almost forgotten. I seem to have been a child who loved to write (I seem to remember that I talked a fair amount too). The story titles are not very inspiring, *The Flood*, *The Holidays*, etc., and the images I used are pretty conventional too; but what goes on inside each piece is alive, even after all this time, to me. It is obviously felt through each pen stroke, and makes me remember the excited precariousness of total absorption. I was writing for my teacher who I felt responded to me, but much more was I writing for myself and the joy of escape. This was something which I have never truly forgotten though much barbed wire has surrounded me since the simplicity of those days. Up until 'O' level I was still legitimately able to write for myself through required English essays, but gradually I had to stop really letting myself go, my emotions laid me open to attack and I became too vulnerable and frightened that what I wrote would be 'wrong'. It was still a great disappointment to me that English 'A' level meant literary criticism only. There was nothing to stop me scribbling away for myself, of course, but time was tight and more importantly I was demoralised. The creative energy I had once possessed seemed to have been overtaken by a creeping paralysis. I remember noticing a book title in the school library *The Death of the Heart* by Elizabeth Bowen, which encapsulated my feelings at the time (I never read the book, it would have destroyed the meaning). I became less and less able to write myself; this is the only personal piece I have written, apart from a diary and two terrible poems, for ten years.

What Melanie is describing from her own experience has been well explored in philosophical terms over the last two decades by educational writers. What she is documenting is the denial of the affective, the suppression of the imaginative, the neglect of the inward, the expressive and the aesthetic. Education in the form of schooling becomes initiation into abstract classification and factual memorisation. Writing becomes a means of objective recording; reading, a means of understanding *about*. Even in the teaching of literature the text can become little more than an object to classify and a smooth path to abstraction. As English teachers we need to find ways of keeping reading in the dramatic and perceptual mode, methods of inhibiting the glib opinion, approaches which encourage that emergent poetic kind of knowing appropriate to literature. But this is to anticipate. First, we must observe the experience of frustration and constriction which the autobiographical passage describes. Secondly, we must note that the experience did not end with 'A' level but continued into University study:

> I floundered about for my three years, learning nothing from the Department except that I disagreed with their whole concept of literature. I became seriously unable to write even critical essays, until I became a write-off as far as the Department was concerned. They eventually dropped my Degree a class because I did not fulfil the essay requirement in the final year (their criterion was numbers not general quality). I tried to leave about five times I think, but it was part of my downward spiral that I could not manage anything so positive as that. Eventually I graduated and it was as if it had happened by mistake. I had tried a million and one approaches for the Department of English, each of my (few) essays charts another stage, but I never really found what it was they wanted, though they said I was close sometimes! The facetiousness is unintentional, it really felt like a game with unknown rules; the great literary tradition they upheld was largely invisible to me. I still never understand how they could justify slotting Blake into some position with a lesser Romantic label on the back of his file.
>
> To return, however, from this totally negative course, I discovered something of myself, for in trying to be what I patently obviously was not, and which seemed hypocritical, I began to have an inkling of the possibilities open to me. I had always known what it was to feel the emotion of the author in any literary work, and to link it to a larger structure seemed at once a way to follow. I knew too how present emotion was in everything I did, and in what most people did too, but now I no longer felt ashamed of this. It was fearfully self-indulgent I suspect but after so long in the dark, a necessary process. People used to make derogatory remarks about women being too 'emotional' but as far as I was concerned this was an added bonus, and one that should be encouraged in all people. My tutors tried to divorce literature from life, and for me *it* failed, and *it* was wrong, if one still needs such value judgements. I realised that I had only to read a novel to be involved in a whole living and creative unity that was far more relevant than a (bankrupt) 'tradition'. By discussion with friends and occasionally tutors, I re-discovered some of this in sharing of ideas about the work – there was no right or wrong, rather an illumination of different facets, each worthy of respect. This was possible through the very process of talking. To me this was vital and I became interested in the primacy of the feeling experience as it occurred, rather than the production of an adequate account of it. I felt I had gone some way at least towards recovering my old excitement for creative writing.

It is not my intention here to evaluate all the judgements made by

Melanie. I only want to claim that in its main drift the argument records a fairly characteristic experience; that, in general, the commentary is eloquently representative. Indeed, when I recently read out the same passages at one of the NATE (National Association for the Teaching of English) Conference commissions I sensed around me a gasp of immediate recognition. Yes, it was immediately felt and subsequently formulated by the English teachers, that was our experience too. For myself, looking back at my own academic experience, I feel I learnt a kind of critical terminology (which was not without value) but that I did not learn that more subtle art of dwelling in a poem, of entering a text innocently, of allowing an experience before formulating opinions. The critical language I mastered (or copied) allowed me to conquer a work intellectually, but it did not let me truly enter it. The approaches fostered by the Department were not sufficiently rooted in the perceptual, associative and imaginative mode, nor did they allow proper existential space for the finding of one's own responses to the texts; and, significantly, there was no space in the formal curriculum for disciplined expressive writing that was not 'criticism'. The tendency was not for creation, contemplation and connection, but more for analysis and dissection. The habit of focused criticism, for all its strengths, precluded that subtle kind of attention without premature conceptualisation which I now regard as the very condition for full literary appreciation. The terminology became a defence against the poem. Before the senses and the imagination had time to recreate the text, the necessary expected judgements were being shaped on the too eager lips.

I put my own criticisms bluntly so as not to shelter, a neutral author, behind my student's autobiography. When I first read Melanie's reflections I recognised them because they defined my own experience and I was impressed by the way in which they located, with such accuracy, the neglected element. The primacy of the feeling experience is what had been overlooked. Clearly any way forward had to release the feeling element, had to consider the structure of the feeling experience as it emerged (beyond any forecast) between the responsive reader and the embodied text. Relationship and experiential meaning – a knowing through feeling and sensing and imagining – must lie at the centre of the enterprise. Indeed, although Melanie did not know D. H. Lawrence's essay on Galsworthy (1928), she was close to expressing the same insights. D. H. Lawrence, it will be recalled, had maintained in that essay:

> Literary criticism can be no more than a reasoned account of the feeling produced upon the critic by the book he is criticizing. Criticism can never be a science: it is in the first place, much too personal, and in the second, it is concerned with values that science ignores. The touchstone is emotion, not reason. We judge a work of art by its effect on our sincere and vital emotion, and nothing else. All the critical twiddle-twaddle about style and form, all this pseudo-scientific classifying and analysing of books in

an imitation-botanical fashion, is mere impertinence and mostly dull jargon.

'A critic', Lawrence went on to insist, 'must be able to *feel* the impact of a work of art in all its complexity and its force . . . He must have the courage to admit what he feels, as well as the flexibility to know what he feels.'

Fidelity to emerging emotional meaning lies at the heart of creative reading, as it does also with expressive writing. I have argued elsewhere that these two activities should be, as in good art and drama courses, closely related; that the sensitive reading of literature and the personal making of literature should be, at points, so intertwined that the insights gained from one flow naturally into the other. I should also like to suggest to the English teacher that in the teaching of poetry (as in the creating of poetry) great, though not exclusive, emphasis should lie on living process, the actual act of engaging with a text, finding representative words for one's own specific though often painfully elusive responses. What is required is the partial restructuring of the teaching of English so that it gives greater space for this existential activity. It is strange, indeed, that with the waning of traditional literary studies we now witness the emergence of structuralism, whose approach, at times, would seem to be even more alien to the development of the intelligence of feeling. From historical studies to linguistics! The movement now needed is one that would link English with the Arts where the study of works has generally run alongside practical expressive work and where immediate authentic responses have invariably been seen as the starting point to emotional and imaginative development.

Melanie's autobiographical extracts thus present us with the problem and, perhaps, also with the key for a further development in English studies. Let us consider what such a development in the reading and writing of poetry might entail.

It would involve, I think, a greater concern in English studies with the individual and collaborative amplification of response to the literary text. The amplification I have in mind allows space for all kinds of initial responses, however naïve, however hesitant, however confused, however idiosyncratic. The comments might refer only to a word or a line which have given delight, or a phrase which confounds or a phrase which seems simply 'wrong'. Nothing which is seriously offered is initially excluded while, at the same time, nothing is definitively accepted. An open space is given for a diversity of response. As the responses develop – here I am envisaging collaborative group work with, perhaps, the teacher as medium and co-ordinator – so they are compared, contrasted, considered, rejected, developed, deepened, modified. The text, in this way, is constantly being returned to at a heightened level of concentration and group participation.

James Hillman (1978) writing in the context of psycho-analysis, has described the practice of amplification as follows:

Sharp definitions are premature. Definitions are anyway more appropriate to logic and natural science . . . Definition settles unease by nailing things down. But the psyche may be better served by amplification, because it prises things loose from their habitual rigid frames in knowledge. Amplification confronts the mind with paradoxes and tensions; it reveals complexities . . . By revolving around the matter under surveillance one amplifies a problem exhaustively. This activity is like a prolonged meditation or variations on a theme of music or the patterns of dance or brush strokes. This permits levels of meaning in any problem to reveal themselves . . .

The art of teaching literature lies, often, in not teaching it at all, but in fermenting a creative unease which releases a multiplicity of authentic responses, associations, reactions, images, suggestions and then slowly brings these back to bear on the text. The teaching begins in negative capability. It begins in a generous sharing of partial responses. It begins in creative amplification. Then, as it moves forward, it seeks a greater accuracy, a greater connection with the text, a greater comprehensiveness but, at the same time, the teacher must keep faith with the experience as it develops among his students or pupils. He must not impose but follow the actual and often unexpected lines of growth as they are stumblingly expressed by the students and, through the searching question or the sudden connecting of seemingly different observations, press them even further. What I am describing is an extremely delicate activity – an activity so complex and multi-faceted it defies full representation. Yet the method of creative amplification – its method and its purpose – is, I hope, reasonably clear. The goal is the establishment of genuine literary judgement through the slow cumulative development of emotional response, collaboratively tested.

Mary Dummett in an autobiographical essay written as part of her MA course at the University of Sussex has described with some care one English teacher who had the ability to allow for the creative amplification of response I am advocating. She wrote:

In the Sixth Form I studied English at advanced level. This course offered both time and opportunity to indulge thoughts and feelings, and the teacher encouraged us to express ourselves freely. We discussed avidly with the certainty of seventeen-year-olds; we argued both eloquently and angrily at times; we felt deeply about every play, novel and poem that we studied. Lessons were challenging and interesting. This teacher knew how to make learning a living process. She encouraged us to express thoughts and feelings *without fear of scorn or a need to give the 'required' answer*. She welcomed an independent view-point *and no matter how unlikely an idea it contained, it was not rejected*. She encouraged us to think critically and independently, to feel deeply and to express ourselves readily and without fear. Original thinking and emotional involvement were not discouraged and consequently *English lessons were occasions when 'self' actually began to emerge out of the anonymity of the institution.* The impact of this aspect of my schooling was, I think, *due to this sense of freedom to explore 'me' – my mind, my senses and feelings –* which the implicit demands for conformity that both home and other aspects of school always inhibit (my italics).

Here we sense the dynamics of true collaborative learning where student, teacher and literary text are brought together. It is precisely this open, engaged teaching/learning activity which Melanie had missed in her experience of English.

We are obsessed with 'right' answers in education. The habit derives from the pathology of technocracy. Yet there are no right answers to be uncritically assimilated in education, least of all in the Arts. No response can be 'right' till it is personal, till it is an authentic utterance. We must, therefore, give our pupils the courage to be naïve, exploratory, honest. Without these qualities the work of literary appreciation cannot begin. But, at the same time, we must not rest content with banalities, catch-phrase reactions, effortless ejaculations. As teachers, we have to find ways whereby provisional first responses can be developed into something more coherent and representative. As I have indicated, the collaborative act of amplification of response to the text is one such method. Another related method is the journal in which initial feelings are jotted down impulsively without care for formal organisation. These notes then form the material for discussion or for a more developed personal appraisal. What we must avoid is the spurious utterance of internalised critical jargon which, so easily, passes for effective criticism. We are out to promote a deeply personal encounter with the text.

Yet the danger remains that it becomes all too conceptual, that the discussion bursts out of the imaginative and dramatic mode and becomes abstract. We have neglected the truth that poetry is physical, excites the senses, feeds the imagination and works, in large measure, through articulated sound. It enters the ear, not the eye. Its rhythmic force is close to the organic rhythms of the body. Too often, we have turned poetry into another abstract entity. I have watched many classes where the poems to be discussed are not even read out. In a powerful essay entitled 'Teaching Poetry' George Whalley (1979) has drawn attention to the importance of reading poetry – a simple observation, but with consequences which are easily overlooked. Whalley claims:

> For educational purposes it is essential that poems be actually heard and listened to, whether as actually spoken aloud or as literally heard when reading in silence. The proper and discrete speaking of poetry provides a double physical bond: we not only hear, but also feel – in the musculature of tongue, lips, throat and face – the physical articulation of the words, the shape, mass movement of the thing.

Having defined the physical and feeling nature of sensitive reading Whalley reflects on his own teaching:

> In my own experience, most students looking at poetry need deliberately to subdue their cerebral anxiety. The first lesson is to engage the senses;

not as an agreeable adjunct to other more intellectual delights, but as the necessary means to hold the mind in the perceptual mode, to keep the habits of abstraction and generalization in their place. Once the senses are engaged all sorts of reflective activities are possible. If that has *not* happened we cannot expect much beyond a feeble pastiche of what is thought to be scholarly behaviour.

But how do we keep the mind in the dramatic and perceptual mode?

One way of keeping the study of the poem 'in the perceptual mode' and of keeping 'the habits of abstraction and generalisation in their place' is by inviting not a critical account of a poem but an expressive rendering of it. Any reading of a poem must represent an interpretation of it. With this principle in mind I recently divided my PGCE English students into groups of three or four, gave each group copies of an unseen poem and then allowed them thirty minutes to prepare an oral rendering. I selected poems with different 'voices' from modern and contemporary poets: Charles Tomlinson's 'Descartes and the Stove', Robinson Jeffers' 'Hurt Hawks', W. H. Auden's 'Refugee Blues' and Elma Mitchell's 'Thoughts after Ruskin'.

For the final reading all the groups came together and were presented with copies of the four poems to be read. Students were invited to comment on each other's renderings, to suggest alternative readings and to justify them. In this concrete manner, reflections on the meaning of the poems were intimately related to the actual verbal organisation of the work, its syntax, its rhythm, its tone and texture. In fact, the text itself will invite some readings, or interpretations, but disqualify others. Some lines cannot be hurried, cannot be given a cynical tone, cannot carry *that* emotion. The specific organisation of the text only allows so many renderings. What is authentically offered and not negated by the whole physical gestalt of the poem remains a valid interpretation.

The central point is that poetry should be *heard* (even when it is quietly read), should be taken into consciousness more through the ear than through the eye. The words printed as black shapes on the page have to be transformed into words shaped on the tongue and, so heard, taken deep into the human imagination. We have neglected the potency of the spoken word. In the classroom and in the seminar we should work to release the oral charge of poetry. We must check the temptation to extract dehydrated 'meaning' from the poem and then discuss that 'meaning' in terms of other solids of meaning. The poem – in all its minute and interrelated particulars of image, rhythm, association, personally recreated in the mind of the reader – is the meaning. Emphasis on the neglected oral charge of literature means that we encourage pupils to record writing, their own as well as that of established authors, on cassettes; that we regularly invite authors in to read their work; that we stock records of poets reading their poems; that we explore the connection between word and musical sound both in direct creative experiment and in such works as, say, *The War Requiem*, where the poet's original texts can be considered in relationship to their musical transformation. All of this serves to keep the study of literature in the expressive dimension.

Wherever possible the study of literature should be kept in some vivid relationship with the other expressive forms, with mime, drama, dance, music, art. How might one convey the mood of this poem in music, in colour, in gesture? How might one represent the feeling of Eliot's four 'Preludes' in paint or sound? How might one convey something of *The Waste Land* through a sequence of dramatic encounters and silent gestures? English, as a discipline, has suffered greatly from its isolation from the other expressive disciplines. Thus many obvious connections between English and the Arts have just not been made in our schools. Because of its unreal separation from the Arts, English has tended to become more and more abstract, theoretical, linguistic or historical, all of which have tended to sever that taproot of poetry descending deep into the body and the imagination of the human being.

The study of poetry in the sensory and expressive mode can be established in different ways. I have referred to creative amplification through informal and collaborative discussion. I have insisted on the release of the oral charge of poetry and tried to give a new emphasis to the actual rendering of poems. I have also suggested that there is a way to literature through channels cut by the other expressive disciplines (and much remains to be done here). But these approaches are not exclusive; for example, Edwin Webb of Garnett College has given me an account of a student-teacher who asked her class to list freely their associations for the following words: rose, worm, night, storm, bed, crimson. Having secured their immediate chain of responses, she proceeded to read William Blake's *The Sick Rose*:

> O Rose thou art sick.
> The invisible worm
> That flies in the night
> In the howling storm:
>
> Has found out thy bed
> Of crimson joy:
> And his dark secret love
> Does thy life destroy.

The exercise in association worked to create a poetic – free, associative – kind of consciousness in the class, and simultaneously, prepared the pupils for the deep archetypal structure of Blake's poem. The exercise was not arbitrary but carefully prefigured the literature which was to be subsequently presented and explored. It forms an excellent example of how the teacher can first engage the poetic consciousness in order to come to the poem more productively. To comprehend the poetic we must work within the poetic.

The exercise in association is also of interest because through its method it implicitly connects the fragments we all carry around somewhere in our consciousness with the organised poem. It is important for the student to sense a continuity between the uncertain, changing, broken details of his own existence and the completed, formal work of literature. Literature grows out of the mess of existence. Literature is an attempt to capture, order, contemplate the complex life which belongs to all of us. 'Classic' should really be understood as 'still remaining vital and subversive' whereas it so often means 'safely dead and buried, guaranteed to give no further trouble'. One of our tasks as English teachers is to lift literature out of the museum and put it back into the market-place. The methods I have described so far are intended to do precisely that, but other approaches are also called for.

One of these is to introduce to our students and pupils selections from more informal literary material: from writers' diaries, letters, autobiographies, interviews, journals. I think, used well, this material can transmit a powerful sense of the urgency of art. It can also foster an awareness of the sources of art-making, of its strange, accidental, mortal origins. Such material asks the student to connect the established work of art with the struggling human being. Let me give a few examples. I should like any fourth or fifth year to know how James Baldwin (1971) described his own experience of starting in earnest to read and write:

> I was looking in books for a bigger world than the world in which I lived. In some blind and instinctive way, I knew that what was happening in those books was also happening all around me and I was trying to make a connection between the books and the life I saw and the life I lived. You think your pain and your heartbreak are unprecedented in the history of the world – but then you read. It was books that taught me that the things that tormented me most were the very things that connected me with all the people who are alive, who had ever been alive. And later, much later, the agony was to translate it – to translate the life that I knew to a page and to give it back. By the time I was fourteen I knew I wanted to be a writer and I wrote all the time. I wrote first on paper bags. I wrote plays and poetry and stories. Writing was my great consolation.
>
> My father said that I was the ugliest child he'd ever seen. He told me that all his life. I believed him, and I accepted that nobody would ever love me. But nobody cares what a writer looks like. I could be as grotesque as a dwarf and it wouldn't matter. For me, writing was an act of love: it was an attempt, not to get the world's attention, but to be loved. It seemed a way to save myself and to save my family. It came out of despair. And it seemed the only way to another world.
>
> I remember the first time I went to the theatre. A white school-teacher had taken an interest in me and she brought me there. And when I saw a real play on a real stage, it meant something. It opened something for me. I began to see that the world in which I lived was not the only world there was. The world she showed me seemed very far away, but it was real. It was there. And then it seemed that maybe it was not entirely impossible for me to reach out to that world.

I should like any Sixth Form studying literature to ponder Virginia Woolf's account of the value of her own writing made in her unfinished autobiographical *A Sketch of the Past* (1939):

> The shock-receiving capacity is what makes me a writer. I hazard the explanation that a shock is at once in my case followed by the desire to explain it. I feel that I have had a blow; but it is not, as I thought as a child, simply a blow from an enemy hidden behind the cotton wool of daily life; it is or will become a revelation of some order; it is a token of some real thing behind appearances; and I make it real by putting it into words. It is only by putting it into words that I make it whole; this wholeness means that it has lost its power to hurt me; it gives me, perhaps because by doing so I take away the pain, a great delight to put the severed parts together. Perhaps this is the strongest pleasure known to me. It is the rapture I get when in writing I seem to be discovering what belongs to what; making a scene come right; making a character come together. From this I reach what I might call a philosophy; at any rate it is a constant idea of mine; that behind the cotton wool is hidden a pattern; that we – I mean all human beings – are connected with this; that the whole world is a work of art; that we are parts of the work of art.

I should want them to compare this with other accounts – from Keats' Letters, from D. H. Lawrence, from Edwin Muir's *An Autobiography*, from Stephen Spender's *World Within World* (where he tellingly distinguishes his own way of writing from that of W. H. Auden). Such excerpts are, of course, not to be used to elucidate a work in a narrow literalist sense, but to indicate the kind of deep existential process which literature manifests.

Furthermore, insights into the creative act can be gleaned from autobiographies and interviews. I should like the Sixth Form also, for example, to consider the following remarks made by the poet Geoffrey Hill. His interviewer Haffenden (1981) asks the question:

> Do you feel, though, that any particular poems were predetermined or preconceived, or is it the case that your insights and concerns always realize themselves solely in the process of composition, in the application of intelligence and technique?

And Geoffrey Hill replies:

> It's a mixture of the two. I've gone sometimes for ten years knowing – in a curiously precise way – that something is waiting to be written; the only obstacle is a total inability to write it. It would be too fanciful to call it a Platonic shape, but I can't think of any other way of describing that strange mixture of nagging and calming allurement – sometimes clear, sometimes hazy, but definitely unattainable for the time being. Then, if I'm lucky, various germinal phrases or a hint of rhythm or something as minutely technical as the cadence of an enjambment will begin to stir, and for a time I have to be content to let the work grow by this process of accretion. Again, if I'm lucky, there will come a point when things begin

to click into shape, and I can push ahead at a somewhat faster rate, but never very fast. I now have a long run of notebooks and, consulting them, I can see how long it has taken in many instances for first ideas to finalize themselves. Such phrases and rhythms and cadences are ganglions in which intellect and emotion and the minute necessary technical adjustments are held together in some way that one knows is full of possibility. But, as I say, for weeks, months, and in some cases years, one cannot discover what that potential is.

It is 'this process of accretion' which our pupils need to become aware of; that just as the making of poetry is often a cumulative, hesitant, impeded movement towards representative form, so the understanding of poetry, invariably follows the same pattern of struggle. Catch-phrase answers are out of court. What we are after is infinitely more subtle, the gradual articulation of personal meaning through the power of the creative word. A study of writer's drafts can be invaluable for revealing the poet's slow accretion of meaning; moving from impulse to tentative symbolism, from tentative symbolism to representative form. I have shown some groups the messy jottings which have been the starting points of some of my own poems and always found it confers confidence: 'You mean you started there. With those clichés and scraps . . . Well, in that case . . .' And that is precisely the point. Frequently the writer begins with what most people have already discarded; sometimes his sources are so commonplace, we had not even noticed them. One of the functions of the writer is to take the ordinary and to work it into significance, to find its hidden archetypal correlative. An occasional collaborative study of sequential drafts can show this process at work. A number of examples can be found in Robin Skelton's *The Poet's Calling* (1975).

In considering the act of writing I am drawn to my final point. The study of poetry and the writing of poetry should be in intimate and reciprocal relationship. The forms studied should be also experimented with by pupils as a possible means for defining their own experiences; the written work of the pupils should be related to what has been achieved in the culture. In this respect English departments would do well to consider some of our best drama and art departments, where expressive practice and sympathetic study run continuously together. The student will respect Shakespeare's or Hopkins' sonnets more highly when he has struggled to convey one of his own experiences through that exacting form. But more deeply, our intention is *to develop the individual's creativity in relationship to all that is given in the symbolic culture.* In the case of English studies, it means that we attempt to draw into a permanent relationship the great creativity embodied in the received literatures (there is now no room for the singular form) and the undeveloped creativity of the individual. I have described in *English Within the Arts* (1982) what this means for the teaching of writing, the various forms which can be introduced and the ways in which this can be achieved. At the most general level, what is required is a much greater recognition of the existential and expressive nature of literature. In this chapter I have tried to indicate how in the teaching of reading and writing these elements may be given their proper weight.

Bibliography

ABBS, P. (1974) *Autobiography in Education* (Gryphon Press)

ABBS, P. (1982) *English Within the Arts* (Hodder and Stoughton)

BALDWIN, J. (1971) 'My Childhood' in *Living Expression* Volume 5 (Ginn)

HAFFENDEN, J. (1981) from 'An Interview with Geoffrey Hill' in *Quarto*, March 1981

HILLMAN, J. (1978) quoted in *The Myth of Analysis* (Harper Colophon Books)

KOESTLER, A. (1964) *The Act of Creation* (Hutchinson)

LAWRENCE, D. H. (1928) 'John Galsworthy' from *Selected Essays* (Penguin)

SKELTON, R. (1971) *The Practice of Poetry* (Heinemann)

SKELTON, R. (1975) *The Poet's Calling* (Heinemann Educational)

WHALLEY, G. (1979) 'Teaching Poetry' in the Journal *The Compass*, No. 5, Canada

WOOLF, V. (1939) 'A Sketch of the Past' from *Moments of Being* (University of Sussex Press)

3 Teaching Drama Texts

Alan England

A chapter on drama in a book recommending an arts-based approach to English studies might to some imply a treatment of those aspects of drama work, as it is currently practised, that make use of theatrical artefacts for educational ends, that encourage the aesthetic appreciation of dramatic language and that involve pupils in the making of plays. But although it was once fashionable to see 'development through drama' as dependent on an improvisatory freedom from the disciplines of art, many teachers of drama now claim that areas of their work outside formal theatre are 'arts-based' and that 'poetic' modes of language do not belong exclusively to the constructs of the playwright. Influential thinkers such as Gavin Bolton, in *Towards a Theory of Drama in Education* (1979), try to establish the terms in which improvised drama activity can be said to offer an aesthetic experience. To do justice to this topic I would need the elbow room of the entire chapter; but for the purposes of the present exercise I shall concentrate on that branch of drama work which, like poetry and the novel, contains an 'invariable' element, a pre-existing schema that focuses the artistic experience and usually takes the form of a script.

However, despite the invariable element, the meanings that can be ascribed to such a script may be infinite. In a sense a play, too, exists only in performance, and its complexion varies with the human individuals who embody it, the human individuals who have a hand in shaping it and the audience who assist at it. As with improvised drama, the words operate in a social and physical context, and their meanings are partly determined by this context. Every fresh attempt has an element of the unpredictable about it.

Such a view has strong implications for teaching method, assuming that the teacher is not hamstrung by the need to train pupils for a literature examination; although, even here, the kind of work I have in mind can provide a marvellous incentive to examine the text and interesting ways to get to know it. It will also be an exercise in appreciation and evaluation as it will be testing the scope for insight into human behaviour which a text makes possible. Ideally, the teacher would not be the authority with the right answers but a knowledgeable fellow-explorer. His approach should be experimental – in a sense, improvisatory – and be aimed at finding acceptable contexts, physical and social, for the words of the play. This will mean allowing his pupils to experience a play as an event which occurs in space and unfolds in time. It will also mean allowing them not merely to write and talk but to act, draw, design and move. As with improvised drama, the teacher will be concerned to relate the fictional context to the actual context, mobilising the pupils' own experience and personal attributes. In organising his classes he will have to use a wide range of groupings, if his pupils are to achieve both the intensity of involvement and the understanding of the wholeness that gives the part its significance. Sometimes they will function as actors, sometimes as directors, sometimes as audience. Sometimes they will be split into pairs, sometimes larger groups, sometimes they will operate as a whole class, sometimes as individuals within the class interacting with the teacher.

What the teacher actually does with any class will depend on the composition of the class. He cannot, like the teacher of improvised drama, offer the material to any group of children and be confident that they will connect at their own level. Some will be able to read well enough to tackle the script direct; others may approach it indirectly, but others may not approach it at all. Within the same mixed ability class, there could be some pupils producing a section of a play, others improvising a version of it and others exploring its themes in situations of their own devising. Actual experience of the text in action may be confined, for some of the class, to being present at an investigatory communal reading and offering responses to a cast which is 'showing' its production. There are texts, though, which are specially commissioned, such as the Hutchinson *Playbill* series, whose words can be wielded with however simple an effect by almost anybody, and it pays the teacher not to underestimate his pupils. The teacher's activities will also be influenced by the nature of the piece being used, its style or individual flavour; and time factors may force him to make some prior judgements about this. Yet, if the process is to be genuinely open-ended, finding the appropriate method by trial and error is in itself an act of judgement.

Of the direct methods of approach, a communal reading is the very least a play needs; but even a reading can be conducted in such a way as to make the pupils aware of the importance of the stage picture, of gesture, of spatial relationships and of pace. Pupils don't have to sit in rows talking to the air or the backs of each others' heads. Any arrangement by which they can locate their interlocutors is an improvement on that. Readers can stand and make significant entrances and exits, sound effects can be added and a ground plan and elevation of a possible set worked out and displayed. Sections of dialogue can be tried out at different paces and with different emphases. The orientation of the teacher's questions is very important. He needs to ask the reader what he would be doing as he said these lines, what he is trying to achieve, who is being addressed, who else is on the stage. Mark Miller (1981) has suggested that:

> The question is not 'What does "Our revels now are ended" mean?' but 'What does Prospero mean when he says it to Ferdinand, with Miranda present, at this particular moment in their lives and in the play?' That will depend, at least partly, on how he says it.

'How he says it' will also depend on who the actor is and who is playing opposite him.

The pupil's ability to interpret a play script will be determined by his previous experience in improvised drama, his exposure to theatrical performances and his familiarity with the rehearsal activities of the stage artist. Without such a background, it may be difficult even to elicit reasonable answers to some of the questions recommended above. It follows that some practical work is at least very desirable. To conduct it a teacher will at least have tried to plug the gaps in his own knowledge and experience; but he does not need to be Laurence Olivier or Peter Brook to chance his arm, any more than he would have to be Ted Hughes or William Golding to teach poetry or the novel.

Straight production work on any epsiode from a play will confront the actor and director, whether the rest of the class are directing a chosen cast or whether the class is working in autonomous groups, with decisions as to meaning. The pupil will be trying out different ways of organising the existing space, with the placing of the audience and the orientation of the action towards it, with the range of expression possible for a particular company of actors, with posture, gesture, movement and grouping and with pace and rhythm. One is not trying actually to teach techniques of acting and directing and it is best to let the pupils become familiar through experience with what particular physical arrangements in classroom or hall or particular manners of playing will do.

Second year pupils working on the enactment of an apparently simple piece such as the sketch by David Campton called *Do It Yourself* will find themselves making choices from a range of possibilities. The sketch is about Arthur, a pompous know-all, and Percy, an accident-prone do-it-yourself enthusiast. Percy is making a large box and Arthur enters and interferes again. It emerges, though Arthur doesn't realise it, that Percy intends the box to be a container for Arthur. Arthur can't resist advising Percy on how to do even this.

ARTHUR: You should have asked for my advice. If you'd asked for my advice I'd have given it. I'd have said, "Lead him up to it gently.'
PERCY: Would you? [*He leads Arthur up to the box.*]
ARTHUR: I'd have said, 'Give him a hand to step inside.'
PERCY: Would you? [*He hands Arthur into the box.*]
ARTHUR: I'd have asked him to sit down. [*He sits.*]
PERCY: How would you nail the lid down?
ARTHUR: With six-inch nails.
PERCY: Six-inch nails.
ARTHUR: And a hammer. Have you got six-inch nails?
PERCY: And a hammer.
ARTHUR: Then I'd slam the lid shut.
PERCY: Right. [*He slams the lid shut. Arthur instantly opens it.*]
ARTHUR: Then I'd nail it down.
PERCY: Right. [*He slams the lid shut. Arthur instantly opens it.*]
ARTHUR: Quickly.

PERCY: [*He slams the lid shut and nails it down, then stands back, delighted and horrified. He smacks the lid defiantly.*]

PERCY: What ought I to do with the box now, eh? What ought I to do with it now? [*The box turns over. Arthur emerges from underneath.*]

ARTHUR: If I were you, I'd put a bottom in.

How does Arthur allow himself to be led to the box? As though he's humouring Percy? As though he doesn't realise it's happening? When Arthur sits, how does Percy behave? Self-satisfied? Kicking himself for not having thought of it? How should the three actions be timed? Does Percy really want to know how to nail the lid down or is he letting Arthur bring the catastrophe on himself? Is it more effective if Percy picks up the objects when he says 'six-inch nails' and 'a hammer' or if he keeps going for them, only to be interrupted by the reappearance of Arthur? How does Arthur say his last line? Is he triumphant at escaping or gloating merely over Percy's inefficiency? At what point does he realise that the box has no bottom in it? How seriously can Percy's resentment and Arthur's presumptuousness be played? How much sympathy can each character be allowed at the end? What are the implications of the different ways of performing? A short piece like this can, without too much trouble, be learned by heart, an achievement which greatly increases the freedom of the participants to experiment.

But in general, however inadequate the ultimate run through of a scene considered as presentable theatre may be, the activity will have quickened, in some small degree, an awareness of the life of the drama and the terms on which its meanings are apprehended. A group able to make a reasonable attempt at reading performance might be encouraged to investigate the style of a piece by deliberately trying out different styles of playing. They might see if the 'China Scene' in *The Country Wife* by William Wycherley could be played in the brittle manner of a Noël Coward comedy. Or does it work best when played with grotesque exaggeration and blatant bawdiness? Straight production, though, may not be the answer with some classes and the teacher may prefer to resort to various other kinds of activity, always, of course, in the experimental spirit.

He may, for instance, decide to focus attention on the physical dimension of the action, whether it reinforces or contradicts the burden of the words. *The Caretaker*, by Harold Pinter, begins with a description of the silent, intriguing actions performed by Mick. After a class reading to establish the broad outlines of the play, small groups can profitably experiment with what Mick can or should suggest by his manner of movement. What is his relationship with the chaotic room or with the people about to enter? What expectations should he arouse in the audience? Should he betray his feelings or present a bland exterior? Only experiment and elimination can resolve this satisfactorily. Suppose the teacher is working on a play which explicitly requires or implies a high proportion of physical action, say *The Second Shepherds' Play* rather than the Hell Scene from *Man and Superman*. He might invite the pupils to join him in searching the text for clues and constructing a scenario for a mime performance. They can polish the mime in groups and offer their achievement for consideration by the rest. The teacher can then cash in on any spontaneous differences in style of playing to raise questions about permissible effect; or he may decide to set up experiments himself, encouraging groups to play for comedy or for tragedy, to play for speed or for weighty slowness, thus testing the limits of particular kinds of tone. With slapstick comedy or with plays like those of Bertolt Brecht, where effects are clear and obvious, one useful device is to freeze the action at salient points like a series of cartoons, each of which makes a statement. Pupils work in advance on the sequence of snapshots, the choice and content of which will reveal their combined intuitions and thoughts about interpretation. With all these approaches, movement will, where appropriate, be married eventually to the words and should help the reading process by supplying a sense of structure and direction. Sometimes movement work on the part of the pupils can be steered by a commentary from the teacher or from an eloquent classmate in the manner of a dance drama. Iachimo's soliloquy when he steps out of the trunk into the bedroom of the sleeping Imogen and sets about memorising the details of what he sees can be treated in this manner. It forces the pupil to 'use' what he hears, and precipitates him into the advanced condition of liberty that an actor enjoys when he no longer has to read and try to express with his body at the same time. One can think, too, of Macbeth's address to the dagger and the peasant's prayer in *Mother Courage*, where Kattrin rises and climbs on to the roof under the provocation of what the peasant says. An effective device can be having the class perform the actions with their eyes shut, as this insulates each of them from premature observation by, and of, the others.

A pupil faced with wielding the words will need to understand both the sense and the implications of what he is saying. Sometimes it helps to focus attention on the conscious and unconscious intentions of the character, on what the character is trying to achieve in the play and what effect the pupil expects the character to have on the audience. Has the character any short-term or long-term goals or objectives, anything he needs, wants or hopes for? It can be worth while collecting all the information given about a character and trying to imagine his off-stage life, as this can help the pupil understand why the character says the things he does. This will probably work better with psychologically elaborate plays, such as plays of William Shakespeare or Arthur Miller, although it can reveal unexpected elaborations in plays such as Molière's. If the presence of a subtext is suspected, pupils could be helped to play it by inviting them to perform a scene with the subtext made obvious and then to perform it again with the surface innocent and the buried life implied. The sense of menace in plays such as Pinter's *The Birthday Party* can be usefully exposed and then disguised in this manner.

The detail of the dialogue is obviously going to be important in the long run, but the pupil must not get lost in it like the pygmy in the long grass; he must be able to get some idea where he is going. He needs to be helped to grasp the structure of what he is tackling. He can set about compiling a list of key 'thoughts' in the form of key lines that will give him a skeleton to work with. In groups, pupils then practise these skeleton dialogues, adding detail from the original as their confidence increases and as they need its support. In fact, merely challenging a Sixth Form to reduce a scene from Shakespeare to twenty or thirty lines can face them with demanding decisions as to priority and meaning. Sometimes the structure of a speech can be discussed by inviting the pupils in groups to distribute the lines according to when a change of tone occurs or when a different side of a personality is to the fore. For instance, in Lady Macbeth's soliloquy, one pupil might be given:

> Glamis thou art and Cawdor and shalt be
> What thou art promised.

Another might take:

> . . . Yet do I fear thy nature,
> It is too full o' the mild of human kindness
> To catch the nearest way.

And so on, the inner conflict being objectified in visible form. A temporary dismantling of a speech can be a useful way of bringing freshness to a choral chant or even to a speech which one character delivers but which is choral in intention. The difficulty for the pupil of individually identifying with the public guilt of the chorus in *Murder in the Cathedral* can be eased by giving him only a line or a phrase to cope with first. There is a wide choice:

> I have smelt them, the death-bringers, senses are quickened
> By subtile forebodings; I have heard
> Fluting in the night-time, fluting and owls, have seen at noon
> Scaly wings slanting over, huge and ridiculous. I have tasted
> The savour of putrid flesh in the spoon.

He savours and learns off his individual line, making it his own, then the chorus are invited to assemble one at a time. The first two say their lines to each other, the next to the assembled two and so on, each delivering, as it were, a fresh piece of news. Then, they repeat the procedure, only this time trying to convince not so much each other but an audience, individual contributions creating a group effect. Eventually, of course, idiosyncrasies will have to be toned down in the interests of the common experience being described; but to start with choral speech can lead to the premature formation of a mechanical tune. Reallocating lines not only to different actors but to other characters can be a useful method of investigating how important character is in any particular play. One may find that in parts of *Waiting for Godot* it seems to make little difference whether Vladimir or Estragon says a line. In plays like *Godot*, where story-line is not a prominent feature, the actual structure can be investigated in action by trying them out with the various sections rearranged in a random sequence.

Pupils should be encouraged to experiment with changing the circumstances in which lines are spoken. Which particular posture helps them say a line in a manner which seems acceptable to them? Let Shylock, at the end of the trial scene, try saying: 'I am content', grovelling on his face; and then let him try it standing erect. Let actors try playing *The Way of the World* lounging on seats or on the floor. Let pupils try delivering the same lines from high up and from low down, from far upstage and from right down near the audience, in the middle of a group and in splendid isolation. When Iachimo tells his story to Posthumus of how he enjoyed Imogen, let the actors try it with just the two characters present and then, as Shakespeare wrote it, with Philario restored to the scene. Where there are specified stage directions in a play, let the pupils try ignoring them or completely reversing them, to see if other ways of playing it are permissible. Where pauses are asked for, let the pupils not only ignore them but try the dialogue with the speeches overlapping.

So far, I have discussed activities which involve the pupils in direct manipulation of the words as given, in attempting to make the words their own, or, as Betty Jane Wagner, talking of Dorothy Heathcote's practice, puts it, in acquiring 'power over material, rather than its having power over them' (Wagner, 1979). There are indirect approaches, too, which can work towards the same end. In a sense, in so far as they are experimental, all these methods, direct or indirect, can be described as improvisatory. The pupil is testing the playwright's words against his own experience and his own perceptions. But the less direct methods often involve a temporary substitution of the pupil's words for the original ones.

Some teachers believe that a short cut to controlling rather than being controlled by a play is to supply the pupils with a synopsis and let them improvise their own version first. One snag about this is that the pupils have only the impetus and orientation imparted by the teacher to go on, and the result may be something not merely more trivial but an artefact with a different meaning. I share John Allen's disquiet (1979) about this kind of activity. What, he asks, remains of Shakespeare when you remove the language?

> The situations he poses amount to very little when you remove the material with which he develops these situations.

Hodgson and Richards sensibly avoid this error. In their book, *Improvisation* (1966), they recommend that the class itself constructs a plan of a scene from the script in terms of a number of signposts indicating the main thread of meaning. The pupils then divide into groups and improvise the scene. They have constant recourse to the text both to modify the guidelines and to add to the detail as it becomes necessary. Thus, the sense of direction makes anticipation and therefore reading easier. It is a method that can work extremely well with certain scenes, scenes which have a reasonably obvious narrative development for instance. I have tried it successfully with a group of Sixth Formers working on Act 1, Scene 7 of *Cymbeline*, the scene where Iachimo gives Imogen his false account of the way Posthumus has been behaving in Rome and attempts to seduce her. Starting from after the departure of Pisanio, we produced the following outline: Imogen asks after Posthumus; Iachimo says Posthumus is enjoying himself; the story of the Frenchman and Posthumus's scorn of him; Iachimo pities Imogen; Iachimo hedges; Iachimo hints about Posthumus's behaviour in Rome; the 'facts' about Posthumus and the prostitutes; Imogen starts to believe it; Iachimo expresses disgust and urges revenge; Iachimo pretends he's been testing Imogen and praises Posthumus; Iachimo makes his request about the trunk. This method is less convenient with scenes which progress by means of links such as the sound or association of words rather than the 'logic' of character motivation, parts of *Waiting for Godot*, for instance, or interchanges with Shakespearean Fools.

Sometimes a mixture of the pupils' own words and the words of the original text can be a useful means of exploring the subtext, the subtext being all that goes on beneath the words as given. A class working on Miller's *The Crucible* might be divided into groups and asked to work on the farewell scene between John Proctor and his wife Elizabeth. Two pupils play the characters themselves, two play their *alter egos*. During natural or stipulated pauses in the dialogue the alter ego says what the character would have added, if he had said all that was going on in his mind. What would have emerged during the following interchange between the two?

PROCTOR:	[*with great force of will, but not quite looking at her*]. I have been thinking I would confess to them, Elizabeth. [*She shows nothing.*] What say you? If I give them that?
ELIZABETH:	I cannot judge you, John. [*Pause.*]
PROCTOR:	[*simply – a pure question*]: What would you have me do?
ELIZABETH:	As you will, I would have it. [*Slight pause*] I want you living, John. That's sure.
PROCTOR:	[*pauses, then with a flailing of hope*]: Giles' wife? Have she confessed?
ELIZABETH:	She will not. [*Pause.*]
PROCTOR:	It is a pretence, Elizabeth.
ELIZABETH:	What is?
PROCTOR:	I cannot mount the gibbet like a saint. It is a fraud. I am not that man. [*She is silent.*] My honesty is broke, Elizabeth; I am no good man. Nothing's spoiled by giving them this lie that were not rotten long before.

Sometimes it might be impossible to say what a character is consciously or unconsciously hiding, and the reasons for this impossibility can in themselves be enlightening. Some of Pinter's dialogue might prove itself to be deliberately mystifying or speeches may turn out quite simply to mean what they say. If this procedure is too elaborate, it is sometimes sufficient to award a character an unscheduled soliloquy or aside at a suitable point.

Depending on your point of view, working obliquely to a text can be seen as either creative or irrelevant. Certainly, pupils are required to be more obviously inventive, and the teacher may be satisfied that a worthwhile educational experience has been undergone, even though the product may, in the end, be of little help to the pupil in engaging with the dramatist's words. However, if the teacher believes there is value in the encounter between the pupil's view and the dramatist's, if he believes that through this encounter a pupil's insights can be usefully disciplined and deepened, then work on a text must be judged by whether it can feed back into and improve performance. Verbal invention will be expected to help in the multi-faceted process that is acting.

Inventing the off-stage life of a character is not a matter of improvising or writing the 'further adventures of' but a way of understanding actions or states of mind that the play defines. Thus Adland's idea (in *The Group Approach to Shakespeare: Twelfth Night*, 1973) of having pupils improvise Viola's encounters with Maria, Sir Toby and Malvolio before she first enters to Olivia can help the actress playing Viola with her manner of entry and her subsequent manner of presenting herself on stage. Sometimes a teacher and pupils may usefully put the characters in situations not envisaged by the author. They may have them talk to each other about the events of the play or talk to outsiders. The pupil-participants may thus be both finding language appropriate to the role and observing the character's contribution from outside. The relevance of the talk, though, will need to be checked by an audience or by the teacher. The teacher may decide to keep the reins in his hands by being the 'outsider' himself. This applies when a character is subjected to an interview, where the interrogator steps in at an appropriate moment in a play and quizzes those involved as to their motives, intentions and opinions. He may prefer merely to keep a watching brief while a group of pupils acts as a tribunal conducting an enquiry into events, such as those, for instance, that occur in the town where *Serjeant Musgrave's Dance* by John Arden takes place.

Drawing analogies between situations in a play and situations superficially more familiar to the pupils is a common and perfectly respectable teaching device to help the pupil personalise the dramatist's experience and to give him confidence. Acting out the parallel situation is a beguiling extension of this, but it can present unexpected problems of application. How easy is it to devise an experience parallel in scale or flavour to any tightly written play? How closely should one try to match the detail of the original? Isn't there a point at which the analogue becomes artificial? David Rostron, in an article in *The Use of English* (1975), concocts the following model for the Hal/Falstaff relationship in *Henry IV*:

> In a coffee bar setting, 'Fatty', an elderly, dissolute former teacher who is intelligent, fond of fun but gone to seed, lazy and prone to exaggeration, has considerable influence over a group of working-class lads who are, on the whole, easily led. One of them, Pete, is more intelligent then the others, and – having an eye on the main chance – he wishes to gain the approbation of Harry, an intelligent and socially superior lad, son of the managing director of a local firm. Harry is a natural leader with an ambivalent attitude to his association with the other youths and 'Fatty'. Together, the group plan and execute a robbery of the two local shopkeepers as they carry their takings to the night safe deposit. Harry and Pete, as a joke, then disguise themselves and easily rob 'Fatty' and the others of their booty.

The comparison is so strained one wonders why a teacher should undertake the labour of constructing it. With the scene from *The Caucasian Chalk Circle*, whose use is described in *Drama in Context*, Dorothy Heathcote takes merely the theme. It is not in fact her concern to lead her students back into the Brecht, but if one followed her example and let one's students have a hand in selecting the themes, such an exercise can provide useful insights into the play. If the teacher and pupils working together construct an analogue just complicated enough to throw light on some aspect of the way a play or a scene works, probably this is as much as they should expect of it. The test, again, is whether it enhances the acting out of the original or the conception of it as an event in a theatre.

Exercises and games are a recognised part of Developmental Drama and they have specific short-term goals. They may create a particular frame of mind; they may promote a particular kind of skill. Used for their own sake, they have the same drawbacks as language exercises in English. The danger, as Marowitz puts it, is that they produce a *'mechanistic* effect – which, of course, has nothing to do with the intentions of art' (*The Act of Being*, 1978). Related firmly to an educational context, they can be valuable, especially if they are offered as a basis for experiment and not used as an agent for preconditioning. The same applies in the teaching of scripted drama.

Movement exercises can be valuable in reminding the pupils that they have this expressive dimension open to them. For instance, practising different ways of entering a room can lead into an investigation of the entrances of Feste in *Twelfth Night* and hence of his function. Voice work, testing the range of inflexions that can be applied to a particular statement, can be valuable if it ultimately throws light on the permissible range of possibilities, for example when Prince Hal, in *Henry IV, Part 1*, replies to Falstaff's invitation to 'banish plump Jack and banish all the world' with the ambiguous: 'I do, I will.' A 'place' game I have used involves small groups of students in miming a scene in a chosen location using a stipulated number of invisible props. The rest of the class have to verbalise the signals they receive from watching this performed, guessing 'where' we are. In a workshop on *Cymbeline*, which I have described in an article in *The Use of English* (Spring 1982), I worked with some Sixth Formers on the section of the wager story where Iachimo examines the bedroom of the sleeping Imogen and renders a detailed account of it to Posthumus back in Rome.

> The immediate question we were trying to answer was how Iachimo and Posthumus were to play that encounter. We framed the exercise in terms of collecting data helpful to the actors. We started by playing a class game. The students sat in a square, facing inwards. Each 'side' looked at the wall and furnishings directly in front of it for a few seconds. Then they were told to close their eyes and when an individual was tapped on the head by me, he had to launch into a description of what he had seen and continue until someone else was tapped. Their aim, now, was total recall but the important thing for them to remember was the effort of concentration it required. We stayed in our square, which became slightly enlarged and set about constructing Imogen's bedroom, searching Act II, Scene 4 for the details Iachimo gives Posthumus of the walls, the fireplace, the ceiling, the bed, etc. and 'placing' them in the central space. I invited a volunteer to perform the actions of Iachimo as he emerges from the trunk and takes in his surroundings while another volunteer steered his actions by reading out Iachimo's soliloquy as a kind of dance-drama commentary. I toyed with the idea of having an imaginary Imogen, as the references to the physical features might prove embarrassing, but my worries were unfounded and we got a real one. As the commentary progressed, the audience watched to see if Iachimo convinced them of his genuine attempt to fix a mental photograph. When he flagged, we reminded him of his experience of the game and of what we had learned of Iachimo's motivation.

Subsequently, we did a class production of the scene in Rome where Iachimo sets out to convince Posthumus that he has indeed been in Imogen's bedroom. It was interesting to note that our Iachimo still physicalised his experience of the room, pointing with rhetorical flamboyance to the various features as he saw them in his mind's eye. This gave the actor playing Posthumus something strong to react against, a dramatic justification for his jealous fury. The real educational pay-off came, though, when a student had the acumen to question the validity of the game itself. Was Iachimo, she asked, in fact engaged in a photographic reproduction of the room; or was he selective, showing a marked preference for Imogen herself? Could this be explained as Iachimo's using her to win his wager; or was it a sign that he was fascinated by her beauty? What function does Iachimo fulfil, after all? The exercise had allowed us to ask relevant practical questions which took us into important matters of meaning.

We owe it to our pupils to make accessible to them the ampler kind of knowledge that comes through enabling them, in a literal sense, to become the play. We create with them events in which the pupils, animated by the text, interact with each other. There will undoubtedly be limitations of time and space in many schools that prevent the constant recourse to practical methods; but even a sedentary class can be helped to acquire a conception of the play as a performance. I have already suggested what might be done with a group reading. Pupils can also become directors who are at their preparation stage. They can do a ground plan for a set, draw an elevation and make a model, giving visual expression to their reactions to the text. On this model, they can plan some moves and groupings. They can divide up the play for rehearsal purposes, thus discovering more about the characters' contribution to the action. They can take any scene and score it for performance, annotating and marking it for tone, atmosphere, structure and pace. They can cast a play from readings or from the comparison of recordings. They can describe the kinds of effect they would like music, sound or lights to produce or, in the case of music and sound, make a choice from examples.

Various media of expression are involved, here, but the many modes of language have the key role and inevitably at some stage they involve pupils in trying to capture in words a personal vision of a shared theatrical experience. Writing about plays is one of the most popular of the sedentary activities, but too much of it tends to be discursive or narrowly descriptive and assumes that all the answers are to be found in the play as an organisation of words on a page. 'Write a character-sketch of Macbeth'; or 'Give an account of what happens in the scene with the witches and the apparitions'; or 'Comment on the comic qualities of the "at home" scene in *Pygmalion*'. Some writing needs to be tied where possible more closely to the play in action, whether in or out of the classroom.Pupils could be allowed to write a description of a setting, taking account of the practicalities and possibilities of a particular stage; they could be allowed to speculate on the problems they personally might encounter if they were to play Beatie Bryant, or to pour out their honest reminiscences of the experience of actually attempting the part in a classroom foray with their group; they might be asked what thoughts they gave or could give to their character while he was not officially speaking or before he came on to enable themselves to stay in role; they might be invited to write a soliloquy of their own for their character; as directors, they might be asked what opportunities for legitimate comic action, delivery or business they foresee for a chosen cast in a scene from *Billy Liar*. To write additional dialogue a pupil has to build on a personal response to the play. For instance, 'characters' writing letters to people outside can both convey excitement and indulge in reflective comment, while shy, introspective characters like Laura in *The Glass Menagerie* can use themselves as audience by setting down their reactions in a diary. Newspaper articles can be written, establishing a wider perspective on local events. Freely imaginative writing ranging outside what is given in the text can record an intuitive engagement of actor or director such as might usefully inspire his style of performance or production. The pupils might go for the 'feel' of a setting, or might write a poem encapsulating a character's view of the world as they conceive it. They should be given a chance to articulate their response as an audience, by writing detailed and graphic accounts of performances and attempting to pin down and hold the fleeting experience. But perhaps it is worth reminding even (or especially) the English teacher that verbalising, whether spoken or written, can at times be superfluous; and that at times the biggest favour he can do his pupils is to let them enjoy their drama in its own terms and as an end in itself. Only he will be in a position to make this kind of judgement.

I have considered approaches enabling pupils to take possession of a play in performance. The full meaning of the activity, however, can only emerge when individual workshops are seen in the context of an engagement with the play as a whole. The precise tactics employed will vary according to the structure and style of a particular play, but the general lines of the following strategy for a first term's work on *Twelfth Night* might serve as a model for other texts as well:

1   Read the play as a class and talk about first impressions, keeping conclusions provisional.

2   Break the play into groups of scenes containing developing relationships, for example those between Orsino, Olivia and Viola or those between the characters involved in the humiliation of Malvolio, or in the plot to precipitate the duel between Sir Andrew and Viola.

3   Let the whole class experiment with the same group of scenes. A 'committee' of directors might produce a scene first. Then groups might tackle the scene for themselves as straight production and pool discoveries about character, theme and style. Work on other scenes might involve a variety of practical approaches including the boldly improvisatory. Where appropriate, written work designed to clarify conceptions of role or ideas about presentation might be introduced.

4   Let the pupils work on other groups of scenes bringing out their cumulative effect on an audience and the means available to actors and director for acquiring a sense of continuity.

5   Re-read the play in class. Discuss interpretations of characters and events. Discuss the merits of the alternative modes of presentation that have emerged in the previous weeks. Agree on a setting for a common production, agree on a style. Work either as a class or in groups on a production of an Act of the play or a sequence of scenes, exploring and discussing the practical problems which arise. Write about contributing to and watching the evolution and presentation of that section of the play. Express your personal feelings about the agreed assumptions.

How much actual practical work is possible in the rest of the year depends on the time available, but communal readings, taking production problems into account, should eventually cover the play as a whole. Pupils can discuss and write about the preparation for and challenges of playing the various roles and the problems a director faces in deciding on the effects he wishes to create – for example, with costumes or music. The meanings an audience might take away from a performance can be discovered by feeding in recordings (sound or video) at a later stage, after pupils have wrestled for themselves with production. A theatre visit is very important if it can be managed, although there may be little choice over when this occurs. The class might themselves present a section of the play to another class.

I suggested in my book *Scripted Drama* (1981) that work on a script should involve pupils in seeking 'acceptable contexts, vocal, physical and personal, for the words of the play and the action specified or implied by the text.' The fruitful interaction of the playwright's vision with the pupil's creates for the pupil an experience which is both artistic and educational, indeed which is educational because it is artistic.

Bibliography

ADLAND, D. (1973) *The Group Approach to Shakespeare: Twelfth Night* (Longman)

ALLEN, J. (1979) *Drama in Schools; its Theory and Practice* (Heinemann)

BOLTON, G. (1979) *Towards a Theory of Drama in Education* (Longman)

ENGLAND, A. (1981) *Scripted Drama: a Practical Guide to Teaching Techniques* (Cambridge University Press)

ENGLAND, A. (1982) 'Our Day Schools for Sixth Formers' in *The Use of English*, Volume 33, No. 2

HEATHCOTE, D. (1980) *Drama in Context* (NATE)

HODGSON, J. and RICHARDS, E. (1966) *Improvisation* (Methuen)

MCGREGOR, L., TATE, M. and ROBINSON, K. (1977) *Learning Through Drama* (Heinemann)

MAROWITZ, C. (1978) *The Act of Being* (Secker and Warburg)

MILLER, M. (1981) 'Shakespeare's Languages, Whole and Unspoiled' in *The Use of English*, Volume 32, No. 3

ROBINSON, K. (1980) *Exploring Theatre and Education* (Heinemann)

ROSTRON, D. (1975) 'Some Approaches to the Teaching of Shakespeare' in *The Use of English*, Volume 26, No. 3

WAGNER, B. J. (1979) *Dorothy Heathcote: Drama as a Learning Medium* (Hutchinson)

4 The Basics and 'Remedial' English

Bernadette Walsh

White eyes that shine because he's black. But that does not matter because we are all the same underneath. I meet him when I went to school.

Gerry (aged 14)

The term 'remedial' has come to be another label for those pupils who are academically low-achievers. By the time they have reached their fourth year in the secondary school, they fit into various, more ugly metaphorical categories: 'the sink-bin', 'belts and braces', 'the returned empties' or simply 'the duds'. A more respectable umbrella term is the 'non-examination group' which unthinkingly echoes David Holbrook's dry term 'the unexaminable'. But whatever the choice of contemptuous label or euphemism, the fact remains that here we have a group of children who often bring problems of attitude and adjustment in their school and learning relationships. Rather than measuring their lives in 'coffee spoons' like Prufrock, the 'remedial' pupil would say, 'I have measured my life in detentions, suspensions, and being "on report", not to mention the hours I spend with my Pastoral Care Tutor.' Furthermore, their numbers are increasing at a worrying rate in certain areas such as our inner cities.

'Remedial' children are those who have lost confidence in themselves and in their work. As far as school is concerned, they may become distrustful of others; some individuals are timid and withdrawn, while others become aggressive, a 'disruptive influence' in the classroom. Often making their position worse by their 'undesirable' behaviour, these pupils withdraw from open contact to live a tenuous life on the outer edge of classroom relationships and attachments. Their failure to relate to school may become for them a severe, if disguised emotional problem. It may also come to reflect critically, I feel, on the quality of relationships that a particular school may be offering to them. Could their inability to form good learning attachments be partly to do with the provision of a heavily objective curriculum for these pupils, which neglects their subjective, emotional development and which suppresses the individual's inner life?

How can we offer teaching relationships and seek out work that may genuinely engage the pupils' sincere interest? For the quality of educational materials that exist at present for these pupils is too often boring and mechanical in the extreme. We cannot follow these; yet neither can we merely opt to be shallowly 'progressive', accepting and echoing the meanest products of mass culture: the poorest kind of television programme; the crudest versions of the 'pop-scene'; the more brutal prejudices about race, sex and politics that are too often reflected quite uncritically by the mass media and which may appear to form almost the sum of the pupils' cultural lives. We need to create conditions in which the classroom is able to develop a positive culture of its own, where personal and domestic and local experience can genuinely interact with 'public' forms of knowledge and outlook.

What Can We Dare to Do?

After describing to a group of teachers on an in-service course how my approach to teaching English to 'remedial' pupils involved puppetry, dance, drama, art, film, music as well as fiction and poetry, one person remarked, 'I suppose it's knowing just how much you dare do with them.' On reflection, this innocent comment appears to hold the key to opening up 'remedial' English – daring to be creative, rather than skulking in patterns of teaching that we know will 'keep them quiet for half an hour.'

'Remedial' education is often founded on the groundless assumption that some children require certain discrete skills so that they can achieve a prescribed level of attainment in line with their peers. Attention is conventionally focused on basic skills of literacy and numeracy through a mechanical, linear approach. This view of 'remedial' education, based on massive injections of out of context language exercises and low grade literature, is inappropriate with children who lack essential confidence in classroom language and in their classroom relationships. We have to devise a curriculum which appeals to their sincere, personal needs; which offers some respect for inner, personal aspects of learning.

It is generally held that a 'remedial' secondary school pupil must be taught 'basic' technical skills such as spelling, basic sentence structure, grammar, syntax, parts of speech, before more sustained pieces of writing can be attempted. It is often held further, that if the pupils cannot read fluently in the first place, then what use is it in encouraging them to have an interest in literature or to enjoy poetry? In practice, this means reading or writing success at a low emotional level, as well as at a low calendar year level – for example, punctuating meaningless sentences such as, 'John saw the dog but it was not barking.' This 'painting by numbers' approach to English has nothing to do with language as personal expression. If we wish the pupils really to possess and use the language, then we must give back to them access to their own experience. Only then may we help them discover their capacity for art-discourse.

To borrow a metaphor from Jung, the teacher must first learn to stoop to draw the water from the pupil's stream of being. Such an approach requires her to start from where individuals are, knowing their achievements, limitations and interests; it means sitting down and finding out what they do, who their friends are, swapping jokes; in short, sharing and contributing to their world. It is in this matter of discovering their peculiar capabilities that teaching becomes a task of personal encounter, rather than resorting to the many pre-packed teaching schemes available on the educational market. One should aim instead to explore issues through a particular relationship in order to enable learners to believe in their own 'being-in-the-world'. Then, gradually, attention to more public and universal issues will come from the learner's personal orientation; in Michael Polanyi's words, 'Personal knowledge is fully determined provided that it is pursued with unwavering universal intent' (1969).

To sum up: the teacher works from a sense of her pupils' individual needs. In seeking resources for the classroom she selects whatever has the best chance of connecting with the pupils' own experience. If she will 'only connect' in this way, then she may hear less often the eternal complaint that 'school is boring'. Eventually, she may only enter the pupils' personal space by invitation. Our relationships, even our very identity, depend on meaningful utterances that are received and understood as meaningful. (See Peter Clough's chapter for development of this view.) Every true language lesson should be then a creative act both for the pupil and for the teacher.

To take an example of the rightness of a particular resource in a particular context: Nicola, a fourth year 'remedial' pupil, asked the teacher whether she would like to have one of her kittens as Nicola's mother was going to drown them. The teacher is reminded of Dan Taggart in Seamus Heaney's much anthologised poem 'The Early Purges'. The poem is read by the class and the teacher asks them, too prematurely in this instance, to produce a similar piece of writing. Until a few weeks before this, Nicola, like the rest of the pupils in the class had been deemed virtually illiterate by most of the other subject teachers. Yet she had already proved to me that she could read and write with quite fair competence. (Her pattern was exactly like that of virtually all the others in her group, in fact. As David Holbrook indicated in *English for the Rejected* (1964), many children can be released with dramatic swiftness from an apparent incapacity to read and write, given the right 'connecting'.) But Nicola declares that she still finds written work difficult, and complains. The teacher adjusts to this complaint by encouraging a spoken response which is recorded on a cassette tape. Nicola's conversation with another girl from the same group enables her to explore both poem and incident with a more confident engagement:

MICHELLE: What do you feel like when you hold them kittens?
NICOLA: They're fluffy.
MICHELLE: Are they fluffy and soft?
NICOLA: Hm . . .
MICHELLE: What does your mother think of them?
NICOLA: She likes them.
MICHELLE: Has anyone else seen 'em?

NICOLA:	Na . . .
MICHELLE:	Hm? What were they like when they were born?
NICOLA:	All slimy and 'orrible
MICHELLE:	What did they remind you of?
NICOLA:	Shit! [*giggles*]

It was not strange that Nicola's description of these slimy creatures should be both personal and also reflecting of Seamus Heaney's poem, since, often by using poetry as a starting point, the richness of the language becomes retained by the pupils so that they can make someone else's expression their own. This is why it is important that we choose the most richly laden language we can with 'remedial' groups, so that they form a sensitive awareness of words. This same poem tempted Sharon to write this recollection:

An Early Memory

A sad morning was when my sister and I was very young. We took our dolls and coats into my mum's room we always played in her room and then my brother came upstairs crying. He would be about fourteen at the time. He said, 'Our Felix has been murdered.' Felix was our cat. At first, I did not believe him and then he said, 'Well have a look for yourself then.' I went downstairs with my sister and I saw our Felix lying there. I began to cry. When dad came home we told him. Dad looked and said he had been shot by a pellet gun. I knew a boy with a pellet gun as well. My father worked at a place where they burn people so our Felix went there but, I will never, never forget it because I loved that cat. It used to come and sit on my legs at night and go to sleep.

(This was Sharon's first draft, with the spelling and punctuation improved by herself after going through the script with her teacher in class.)

In this account, the viciousness of the attack on a beloved cat makes the pain felt by the writer more acute. Sharon has managed to convey economically, not only the reaction of the family to the death of a cat, but also details of the family itself – their childhood play, their father's occupation, the unashamed dismay of the older brother. Then there is the initial anxious disbelief at the wickedness of the deed and by contrast, the father's comparative calm practicality as he disposes of the cat; until finally, with one emphatic repetition, Sharon's anguish is revealed when she admits, 'I will never, never forget it because I loved that cat.'

'Do we *have* to write, Miss?'

Once the relationship is formed, a common observation made by those involved with 'remedial' groups is how individuals find difficulty in sustaining pieces of writing, while verbally they may possess a language which is full of vitality, sensitivity and which shows a potential for deeper meaning and understanding; yet there is a reluctance to commit their experiences to paper. They do not need the art of writing to sustain their relationships outside the classroom. Only a truly valued relationship with the teacher can provide the right impetus.

We know that in order to distil an experience in writing, which is so permanent and objective in character by comparison with talking, it is necessary to order the experience in the mind – to reconsider and rearrange it in a form appropriate to the written word. 'Remedial' pupils find it difficult to order experience with sufficient clarity to write about it, often it seems because of their closeness to the experience itself. While the pupil is thinking about and talking about the experience, the experience is in a sense simultaneously present in the mind as a clear, often exciting, sometimes fearful, recollection. By contrast, writing becomes detached and depersonalised when it can no longer capture the enthusiasm of the remembered experience. The linear qualities thus appear to contradict the richness of the experience, in narrowing it down to a mere succession of events. To illustrate the problems and to show some methods employed in overcoming them, passages from my teaching journal are given below:

Monday 19 January
Chris was reluctant to work, complaining that he was too tired. He preferred to look through a pile of examination papers situated near to his desk. He offered to put the papers in order for me – actually this saved me from a very awesome task. Then he demonstrated how his history teacher sat on a desk; after this he settled down to write about his experience at an old people's home. Nearing the end of the lesson and all he had written is 'Got up at 8.30. I went to school and did some lessons. I went home for my tea then I went for a fag and came back in and saw T.V. Then we all went to bed.' Chris jumped up to collect the books and role-played a teacher: 'Stop talking! Sit down and get on wi' yer work!' (Is this stereotype the only impression we as teachers give to these pupils?) What did Chris experience at the Old Folks Home? He hasn't revealed very much, must ask him about it tomorrow. How can I help him to make his writing less mechanical?

Tuesday 20 January
Today we changed rooms for our lesson and Chris was particularly 'fidgety', saying that he did not feel like working but wanted to sit. Unfortunately, he did more than sit as the next moment his desk collapsed – he had unscrewed it from underneath. Rather than show annoyance, I felt that he was just putting me to the test so I said calmly, 'Kindly put the desk back when you've mended it.' Why does even the slightest change in routine make this group react this way? They really need stability. In the afternoon, Chris wanted me to do him a favour – supplying him with a new geography book so that he wouldn't 'get done' for not going for one himself. Felt guilty for refusing at first as I thought, 'Why should I, after this morning?' Hope tomorrow will be different. He still hasn't written a decent piece of work this week.

Wednesday 21 January

I feel I have failed Chris as much as he has disappointed me. So I took him to one side and said positively, 'I know you're wanting to work well to please me in English today, so here's your new book that you wanted. By the way, will you collect the books from the stock room for me and while we walk down, tell me about what you got up to at the Old People's home on Monday.' 'All right, Miss,' Chris came back and I continued to talk to him, and occasionally asked him to jot his notes down. He worked well, but not without sniffing, complaining of a cold, 'Have you got a snot-rag, Miss?' I am increasingly aware of being put in the role of teacher-as-provider – a kind of 'good-enough teacher/mother'? What he wrote was much improved as a result of talking it through first.

> 'I went to the Old People's Home on Monday. Mark and me had a good time up at Willowcroft Home because that is what it is called. Me and Mark got on a bus outside our school we got off outside the Old People's Home. We went in and a lady said, "Hello". She was very nice to me and Mark, she said go and talk to the people so me and Mark went and was talking to the old people. There are a lot of old people in the home because we went in about four or five rooms. We went in one room and we was talking to an old lady and we had a laugh or two. They're was a lady who was small and old, there was four or five men in the old people's home. A lady had a stroke and all she could say was I and I was talking to her and she was saying I all the time but I did not know then but a girl came and said "That lady had a stroke and all she can say is I." so me and Mark went into the next room and a lady say to Mark you are a blackman and me and Mark got away from her because she was in a very bad mood. After that it was 3.30 and they all jumped up and said Tea Time but it was not till 4.00.'

Chris then read his account to Mark. I hope this will encourage Mark to write a similar response.

Thursday 22 January

I knew Chris would not wish to be 'outdone' when Mark wanted to use the tape recorder so the pair of them gave further discussion over their Old People's Home visit. They seemed impressed by the print I took in to start them off – Halina Dabrowska's 'Old Woman with a Cat'. Mark said it reminded him of 'Willowcroft'. By the end of the lesson he had laboured over the following written record of his visit:

> 'I and Chris went to the Old People's Home as soon as we got there a woman showed us around and introduced us to everybody. They were all plesant and nice to know we said hello to them and we all had a cup of coffee and we all sat watching T.V. I read the newspaper. When we arrived most of them was a sleep but we soon got them on there feet springing about. Then two girls from a nother school and they had a radio so we all got the residence dancing till it come to dinner time when we had to go. I did not want to go but Chris was in a hurry Chris said to them do you want to write to anybody and it made me sad when one said we have got no one to write to everything went quiet so I told them a joke to cheer them up then we went. I could tell they did not

want us to away they all came to the door and wave. Any way I enjoyed
my self and I think they enjoyed there self too and hope to have us back
soon. The End.'

I notice that Mark doesn't mention the woman's comment that he is
black, as Chris recorded – hope he wasn't upset. It may be a time to raise
the issue of racial prejudice – could use Wole Soyinka's 'Telephone
Conversation'. Must check up on Paula Modersohn-Becker's paintings;
she has one depicting a white child and a black child embracing – called
'Madchen und Knabe aneinandergelehnt'.

These diary extracts dwell on the contrast that a teacher often finds
between the liveliness of spoken recollections, and the flat, broken
sentences that characterise first attempts at writing; Chris's written
impressions here present themselves in undifferentiated confusion.
How are the 'remedial' pupils to select, order and phrase their often
richly complex, many-layered images? How can their immediate
subjective, personal experience be presented for more public recognition? How can we help Chris to develop his flat, mechanical effort to a
more meaningful, feeling attempt?

First there has to follow a period of 'sorting out' which can involve
another creative art-form such as talking on to a tape, drama in the form
of role-play or improvisations, dance, sculpting or a quick sketch or
painting; in fact, any form of expressive discipline can be used before a
written form is attempted. For example, Mark and Nicola, after walking
through the woods, sketched the waterfall that they saw before
attempting to write a poem.

Friday 27 March
Although the school is only a mile from the city centre, we are
surrounded by extensive parks and woodland; and it's Spring. The day
was so fine that I decided to let the group go outside. I had intended to
continue with Seamus Heaney's 'An Advancement in Learning', but the
weather dictated the order of the day. I told the group that we were
looking for signs of Spring and we would note what we observed. The
boys, immediately we were outside, hid in the bushes; I had expected this
and had to laugh at their antics. They delighted in calling to me, their
shouts echoed through the woods. Near the gardens was a hen-coop: it
surprised the girls to learn that this was where hens lived! We noticed that
the stream was almost bursting its banks and that the waterfall was
overflowing because of the exceptionally wet month. It must have made
an impression on some of the group because Nicola and Mark wanted to
sketch the waterfall. Mark hid under the bridge and said we couldn't
cross as he was the Billy Goat Gruff! The dried up lake was the next area of
fascination – 'Look at Chris, Miss, he's trying to walk on t'water.' In the
middle of the mud was a clump of pussy-willows. Mark waded out to
strip a twig for us to take back to class. Later, the girls arranged some
blossom in a vase . . . follow-up work seems inappropriate now, since the
event was itself a celebration.

Monday 30 March
The weekend gave me time to 'dig out' a few pictures showing waterfalls and I've bought a film for the camera. Mark can try his hand if he wants to; he'd much rather photograph the waterfall than write about it. I also needed Robert Southey's 'Cataract of Lodore'. The lesson was very quiet. Chris needed help to start his writing on a story entitled 'Fear' and said, 'Go away, Miss, I've got it all together now.' He worked with great concentration and wrote the following:

> When I was a child I was shy and need the protection of the family I used to go to school and when the teacher said something I used to go red I sometimes go red now I feel daft sometimes and people think I am mad.
>
> A long time ago, I can't remember much, but I can remember chasing a rat round our front room in our old house which we don't live in anymore. I can remember falling out of bed too and I was sitting in the pram biting the rail and fell out and hurt my lip but I think that it was really my mum and dad telling me about that memory.
>
> I used to call our cat a dog because I thought it was one and once I threw it on the fire and my mum said, 'What have you thrown the cat on the fire for?' I said, 'I thought it was cold so I wanted to warm him up.' she pulled him off and he had only singed his fur.
>
> I remember going to our corner shop to buy licorice allsorts, licorice sticks, fizz bombs and that's all the woman used to give me.
>
> I remember a dream once, I was in bed one night and dreamed that I got up and there were rats all over the floor and I stood on a load of rats and there was blood on my feet. In my dream I woke up and the rats had gone, and mum said,
> 'What have you got blood on your feet for?'
> 'I've killed the rats,' I said.
> 'What rats?'
> 'They've gone! They've gone!'

Chris has placed his own unique stamp on this writing; but it also contains remarkable echoes of Seamus Heaney's 'Advancement in Learning', in so far as both are records of a childhood experience in which the writer overcame fear, metaphorically epitomised as rats. Must read this poem to Chris. Sat with Mark and Nicola to help them sort out their ideas for a poem on the waterfall. These were their immediate written responses:

Waterfall

The waterfall was frozen over from
the Winter time but now it
Burst into life like Spring
it has started running again
fast, bright water like melting snow
icy, cold and fresh
running downstream over
rocks and stones.

Nicola (aged 14)

Waterfalling

dripping
sparkling
water bouncing off the stones
reflecting and catching the
light
trickling
bubbling
rushing
hissing
clamouring and clambering over
the rocks.

Mark (aged 14)

Before such writing could take place, it was essential to encourage the pupil to talk about the experience, to describe in detail no more than a single incident or impression, a significant moment rather than a sustained sequence of events. The spoken anecdote is then translated into the more self-enclosed and formalised medium of writing; but often technical limitations complicate and frustrate what the pupil wants to write. To overcome this problem, it is helpful if the teacher herself writes down the pupil's dictated words, probing all the while for more telling phrases as the experience unfolds itself; but these must come from the pupil. Questions such as 'What did it look like . . .?' 'What did it feel like . . .?' 'Then what happened . . .?' 'What did you think and feel about it . . .?' can help pupils to sort out these impressions into a coherent form. Mark, who always found difficulty in writing down his thoughts, produced through this technique a poem similar in feeling to W. B. Yeats' 'Squirrel at Kyle-Na-No'; yet the poem was derived not from literature but entirely from his own observing of a squirrel in the local park:

Squirrel in the Wood

Little squirrel
jumping from branch to branch
I see a flash of bushy tail
grey, brown
little squirrel
where do you collect nuts?
why leap through the trees
As if I was going to hurt you?

Mark (aged 14)

Because of the artificiality of the task, 'remedial' pupils find writing difficult; but if they are encouraged to enlarge one vignette of experience in the form of a poem or short paragraph, writing becomes less daunting. It is then easier for them to keep within the limits of their own technical ability in respect of vocabulary, spelling, syntax, handwriting and overall length. In this way as much complexity of feeling as possible about the experience is concentrated into the writing; perhaps Jane Austen's words best summarise this when she speaks disclaimingly of 'the little bit of ivory on which I work with so fine a brush as produces little effect after so much labour.' Even at this stage a teacher will receive writing from the individual where spelling may be erratic to say the least; but at last there can be concrete improvement here because there is something that now awaits editing – which should be a far more meaningful task than mechanical exercises can allow. As with all art, there has to be a discipline; and this writing attempted by the 'remedial' pupils represents considerable effort as their attempts become nurtured into a coherent form. But it is only when feeling plays a part in learning that such pupils will feel encouraged to work with tenacity to improve their performance. It is clear that many 'remedial' pupils see themselves usually as low achievers, and this has a depressing effect upon their motivation and their view of themselves as group members. They are in danger then of falling helpless into ruts of under-achievement. Correspondingly, any success, provided it is quickly recognised and shown to be valued by the teacher, contributes to counteracting these feelings. As confidence and trust in the teacher, and in each other grows, so diffidence disappears. The teacher's personality will also become mediated in the work of the pupil-artist, who will gladly draw on all the cross currents of contact and relationship that become available in a classroom where language has a living context.

When the teacher is working from the known experience of the pupil towards the unknown, this often involves her in having to provide or re-enact for the pupil an enriching experience in the first place. Ideally this should be at first hand and explored initially through the senses. This often means abandoning pre-planned lessons to live for the richer moments of a sudden snow-storm, flash of lightning, torrential rain, the sound of fire-engines which enter the classroom daily without invitation. For example, Mark produced these few lines on seeing a magpie in the playground.

Magpies

One for sorrow
Two for joy
Magpies
Two magpies
There he is
There he is
Near the football pitch
Walking around pecking
The ground for bits
What joy will they bring?
What sorrow?

Mark (aged 14)

A glut of apples in autumn provided the group with another starting point. With the simple request that they should munch as they wrote, Chris produced a statement that was full of an awareness of the interplay of the senses:

Apple

The apple shape is round
the taste of the apple is mouthwatering
The colour is green and red
I crunch into the apple
and it smells like cider.
I had a very big bite
not a crunch.
But the juice stops me eating
I think I should have a bite
again but when the air gets to it the
apple went brown but I bit and bit
until it was all gone so I stopped and
just left the apple core.

Chris (aged 14)

This type of work may be said to be typical of a bright top junior. It may also be said to be typical of anyone who has ever eaten an apple with conscious pleasure. For Chris, it is a perfectly fresh statement that he has never felt able to attempt before in writing. Such an experience can then be coupled with another poem or prose extract, in order to show that even experienced writers feel the same as themselves; this poem by Chris for example was displayed alongside Laurie Lee's poem 'Apples'. In short, it is ineffective to ask 'remedial' pupils to 'write about blackberry picking in Autumn' if they've never experienced it. If because of the normal constraints of the school-day it is impossible to take the group out occasionally to let them become aware of the environment, then it is the responsibility of the teacher to bring the environment into the classroom however simply, so long as the attempt is sincere. One example of this is the following transcript of a lesson taped during a class response to a cutting of lavender which I had taken in to show them. I feel that it clearly shows the delight of the pupils in experiencing sensually the qualities of this particular plant.

ANTHONY: What's that?
TEACHER: Does anyone know what it is?
NIGEL: Plant.
JOHN: A wild one.
ANTHONY: Deadly.
ANDREW: Lavender.
ANDREA: Heather.
TEACHER: Pardon?
ANDREW: Lavender.
TEACHER: Heather? Thank you, it's lavender, yes, and what does anyone know about lavender? Anyone?

ANTHONY:	It smells.
PAUL:	Smells.
TEACHER:	It smells. What do you make it into?
ANDREW:	Lavender bag.
TEACHER:	Lavender bags. What are they for?
MARIA:	Putting in your wardrobe.
TEACHER:	Why?
ANDREA:	To make your clothes smell.
TEACHER:	What are they used instead of?
DEBRA:	Perfume.
TEACHER:	Perfume, yes. What did people used to put in their wardrobe in the olden days?
ANDREW:	Mothballs.
ANTHONY:	Moth – what?
TEACHER:	And these . . . mothballs. And why did people put things in their wardrobe?
PAUL:	To keep their clothes smelling nice.
DEBRA:	Smell nice.
PAT:	Keep their clothes nice.
NIGEL:	To stop their clothes going fusty.
TEACHER:	Yes. Right, can anyone think of any descriptive words that we could use to describe this?
ANTHONY:	A weed.
ANDREW:	Green.
TEACHER:	Green – you think it's green. All right, that's a colour.
ANDREW:	Green and a bit of buds.
TEACHER:	Buds? Yes.
JIMMY:	A mess. [*Group laugh, teacher guides him towards a closer examination of the plant.*]
TEACHER:	Jimmy, if you press that there at the top then . . .
JIMMY:	It's brilliant.
TEACHER:	What does it smell of? What does it remind you of?
JIMMY:	Erm . . .
ANDREA:	Smell at your fingers.
JIMMY:	Er . . .
JOHN:	Pooh! I got it up me noowuz [nose]. [*Laughs.*]
TEACHER:	Anyone else?
ANDREW:	Air freshener.
TEACHER:	Air freshener. All right. Sometimes they have that . . . what words describe the shape? What words describe the shape?
ANDREW:	Tree-like.
ANDREA:	Like a tree.
TEACHER:	Bushy. Like a tree.
DAVID:	Like a bush.
TEACHER:	Like a bush, bushy, good, what else?
ANDREW:	Spikey.
TEACHER:	Spikey; that's a good word. What about the colour?
ANTHONY:	[*disguised voice*]: Hold it, spikey!
JOHN:	Green.
TEACHER:	Are you sure about that?
JIMMY:	Greenish, greenish white, like snowy-white.
TEACHER:	Like snowy-white, that's a good one.

JIMMY: Still smells. [*Andrea smells and coughs.*] Miss, it smells like fly-killer.
TEACHER: Like fly-killer.
ANDREA: Sh-sh. [*Imitates sound of aerosol.*]
JOHN: Think if I were a fly near that, I wouldn't shift ageean (again).
TEACHER: Why not? [*Group examine plant and talk about it together*] All right, think about the smell, does it remind you of anything else except air-freshener and . . .
ANTHONY   Ah . . .
DEBRA: Ay! Them sweets . . .
PAT: Palma violets.
TEACHER: Which sweets . . . Palma violets? Ah yes!
ANTHONY: Palma violets?
TEACHER: Let's see if we can put some of these ideas on paper and we'll write something about lavender. . . . .

The jokes, teasing, verbal interplay and the sense of fun in the air are all signs of their quickened interest. Whoever brought lavender into their classroom before? They became engaged in learning play, almost unawares. Their initial reactions also emphasise the creative role of talk as a way through which future, more sophisticated, forms of writing can be prepared, as these attempts indicate:

A Scent of Lavender

The smell of the lavender
is like an air-fresh spray
but still the smell is not very pleasant.
When you first get up in the early
morning the scent of lavender
hits you in the face.
Then, after a while the smell
is quite pleasant
As you go down to breakfast
the scent hovers over
the breakfast table.

Jimmy (aged 14)

Lavender Blue

Lavender blue, deep blue
pale green and grey
it has a strange smell which lingers
on the fingers of
a gardener in an old lady's stately home.

John (aged 14)

Teaching thus from a capacity for all knowledge, the teacher draws from the richest bounty that she knows and takes an active interest in the words of the pupils she teaches – she is aware of which team won the match at the weekend, as the result will influence the mood of the most ardent fan; she is aware that someone is going to buy some shoes this evening after school; she is aware that someone is celebrating a birthday; she is aware of her pupils as people.

The role of the teacher is seen then to be a provider and a willing receiver, an enabler and trusted friend rather than an inhibiting 'corrector' of expression. In a warm, sensitive climate, one which is rooted in trust and encouragement, the emphasis falls on the creative process rather than on a measurable skills performance. The pupils are valued not for how 'productive' they are, but for the quality of the lived experience that is to be told – a combination of memories, perceptions and anticipations, thus unifying knowing and living. Art-language is seen as the process by which meaning is articulated, by which knowledge becomes personal. Two pieces of writing which I have come to value serve as examples of this. The first is a boy's memory of his grandfather. Deliberately, I present it in its raw state to show that when feeling is present, felicity of expression somehow seems quite inseparable from a simple, pure respect for the truth of things:

> My grandfather was the best friend I had. He was the one who looked after me when I was young. Then when I started to grow up he was the one who had the most incomon withe me. We shared the same interests. We would spend hours studying the betting forms of hourses discusing there chances working out there folts then he'd go and back an twelve to one outsider and blow me if he didn't collect.
>
> Mind you he was'nt all good he had his folts too. He had his littel petty dislikes for egsample if he ever sawre an asian or a black person walking down the road you could bet your lif he'd say, 'Bludy imigrants' wether they were english or not it did'nt matter to him but that's how it goes.
>
> Anyway when someone was as good as him you tend to forget that you had your dislikes about them. I rembere a time when we were playing cardes it was a Saturday night and we'ed won all the nabours money of them so they'd gone home in a mood.
> 'Shall we carry on son' he said to me with a wink
> 'Okay then if you promise not to cheat,' He giggled girlishly then agreed. I made a cup of coffee then he delt the cards. There was all the money in the pot when we'd finished betting and he'ed agreed to throw the cardes when he did I couldn't beleave he'ed cheated but could not bring myself to acuse him.
>
> For the next few days he was drunk and I had to carry him to bed and leav him there.
>
> There were plenty of uther ocations when he cheated me out of money when he lied to me and when he hit me but for all this he was the best friend I ever had and may he win the wings of the angels as he used to say.
>
> *Simon (aged 15)*

It did not take Simon long to make a second draft of this after the spelling and punctuation had been tidied up. The second piece was the result of finding out that one boy in the class was a moto cross enthusiast. For some time the fear of errors of spelling and punctuation had paralysed his writing until he had been fully assured that once he had something meaningful to write, spellings and so on would eventually 'look after themselves' The following 'tidied up' attempt shows the depth of Andrew's 'oneness' with bikes, and in his attempt to convey this feeling his powers of expression improved:

Moto Cross

The bike stands new gleaming
gold rimmed wheels.

Silvery chromed forks and suspension
The black rubber of the wheels
wet reflective in the morning dew.

The white plastic of the panels,
mudguards and tank.

The black metallic engine
with leads and pipes growing
from its tarnished surface

There it stands – quiet, cold
stationary in the damp
grass of the almost empty field.

The crowds came
the field brimmed with people.

The rider approached and
sat astride his calmed beast.

The excitement of the rider
built up – so did the crowds.

As the rider started his beast
he felt as if his
bike and himself
were being moulded into
one.

The invincible force . . .

Andrew (aged 15)

At the centre of any 'Remedial Education' there must be such an 'art-language' to express and communicate each learner's inner needs. It must be presented within the context of a sympathetic relationship with the teacher otherwise the 'remedial' child's plight could be epitomised by another of T. S. Eliot's anti-heroes, 'We had the experience but missed the meaning.' Rather it is a relationship which can only be called a form of love – a love which insists that there should be exchange of meaning between the partners of that love.

English teaching is indeed concerned with 'basic' skills; it is concerned with providing conditions in which learners can make the effort through words to fit meanings, personal and public. The term 'basic' ought to direct us back to the foundation of language – to that which is beyond words, which is life itself. Meaning is an intention of the mind; and to borrow Polanyi's analogy, we should look beyond the point of the finger-end (the words) to where it points (the experience), in order to share meaning. If we can look for living forms in our teaching, the structures of language will form themselves well enough around them. For 'remedial' pupils, as for us all, language should be a personal possession, revealing and communicating the quality of their humanness.

Bibliography

HOLBROOK, D. (1964) *English For the Rejected* (Cambridge University Press.)

POLANYI, M. (1958) *Personal Knowledge: Towards a Post-Critical Philosophy* (Routledge and Kegan Paul)

POLANYI, M. (1969) *Knowing and Being* (Routledge and Kegan Paul)

WINNICOTT, D. W. (1971) *Therapeutic Consultations in Child Psychiatry* (Hogarth Press)

5 Choosing and Presenting Fiction for Younger Classes

Helen and Colin Pearce

We both teach and believe in a literature-based English syllabus. That is, we encourage the reading of literature from the first year in as many ways as we can; and we accept the wider, umbrella term 'arts-based' as it is being used in this book. What is it about children's fiction in particular that we feel is strong enough to base much of our English teaching of younger classes upon it? And what criteria do we use to choose those books? We shall look briefly at these questions, before discussing strategies for opening up books to younger readers and concluding with extracts from a half-term's outline of work to accompany a recommended third year reader, Louise Fitzhugh's *Nobody's Family is Going to Change*.

The core of our reading programme is the class reader, though it would be wrong of us to suggest that we do nothing but teach class readers. We encourage the reading habit in private reading lessons each week. We use themes and ideas from fiction as the stimulus for many drama lessons. We employ the books we are reading in class to develop language use in writing and talking. We try to encourage children to write longer pieces of imaginative work, formulated into chapters and showing a coherent development of characterisation and narrative. Also, some of our English teaching consists of shorter pieces around a central idea – a topic, or short story, or 'theme', which is explored and developed in successive lessons.

If we claim that children's fiction is a worthwhile basis for English studies, we need also to acknowledge that some books will be better than others, for classroom use. First, the books we choose have to be interesting and accessible to young minds as well as being educative, though they do not have to be either moralistic or solemn. In fact, in the early years we tend to choose stories and novels rich with humour. In the first year our choices might include *The Balaclava Story* by George Layton, Barbara Robinson's *The Worst Kids in the World*, Betsy Byars' *The Midnight Fox* and *The Eighteenth Emergency*, and Robert O'Brien's *Mrs Frisby and the Rats of NIMH*.

In the second year there is *Grinny* and other science fiction by Nicholas Fisk, *Conrad's War* by Andrew Davies, *The Trouble with Donovan Croft* by Bernard Ashley, and one of Nina Bawden's best books, *Carrie's War*.

In the third year the whole field begins to open up with the adolescent-conscious American books like Paul Zindel's *The Pigman*, S. E. Hinton's *The Outsiders* and Louise Fitzhugh's *Nobody's Family is Going to Change*; and for the more mature, Rosa Guy's *The Friends*. Among native writers there is the social realism of Barry Hines' *A Kestrel for a Knave* and *Joby* by Stan Barstow, the almost universal appeal of Robert Westall's *The Machine Gunners*, J. R. Townsend's *Noah's Castle* and Alan Garner's *The Owl Service*.

It would be impossible here to give full reasons for all these choices, but one might be taken from each year by way of illustration: *The Midnight Fox*, *Carrie's War* and *Nobody's Family is Going to Change*. We want children to enjoy and understand what they are reading; to see books as pleasurable; to inculcate the reading habit; to try to counter the dramatic decline in reading during later adolescence. We want these books to provide the valuable imaginative projection and wish-fulfilment that can be gained from fiction, as well as providing a means by which the pupil can be what Denys Harding (1937) called an 'onlooker', contemplating the treatment of action, character and ideas in the text. Without a background of fiction to 'enlarge . . . understanding of the range of human possibilities' in the words of the Bullock Report (1975) children are in danger of leaving school fundamentally deprived, not because they are without a key to that fabled 'culture' cupboard, but because to lose books is to lose what amounts to a kind of sixth sense, or faculty.

We are aware that two out of the three books chosen for special attention are American. This might give cause for criticism, but what we enjoy from these books are their qualities of sharp dialogue, their wry sense of humour, their tactful yet unabashed handling of adolescent problems (or what adult writers feel are adolescent problems). We would not, of course, suggest an entire diet of American novels, or suggest that the qualities listed above belong to American novels alone. We have chosen these books on their own individual merits, regardless of their origin, because they contain the kinds of contexts and emotions which will challenge the reader's expectations.

The Midnight Fox uses humour throughout to good purpose, and, in its own light way challenges harmful sex-stereotyping while focusing on a city boy gradually becoming aware of nature and its harshness, through his fascination with a fox. The novel takes the time worn theme of child befriending animal against man; and despite the danger of sentimentality inherent in this formula, preserves good humour and common sense. The city boy, previously obsessed with the pastimes of a technological society, and downtrodden by his parents' concern for his psychological development as a 'real boy' is not lacking in sensitivity, but in some real outlet for his concern and caring. The overall theme of parents' expectations, and the unhappiness caused to children when they cannot fulfil these, is used to humorous effect. The parents' expectations and conventional notions are gently ridiculed and undermined in the face of the child's appreciation of an animal's fight for survival.

There is a shift in criteria with the choice of *Carrie's War*. Here we have a novel of historical interest, based on the evacuation of children from cities during the Second World War. Nick and Carrie are displaced from their own familiar and comforting locale and are forced into a perhaps premature awareness of adulthood. Carrie bears the real burden of these experiences, and we see at the beginning and end of the novel how this has marked her as an adult. Nick is the touchstone of childhood innocence (and selfishness) remaining splendidly untouched by events. Nick has no real desire, or ability, to change events; Carrie on the other hand has both – but has to pay the price as she becomes aware of the many wrongs inflicted by adults upon one another. But this may suggest a too sombre account of a novel which is written in an entertaining, often gripping way; and which recognises the ability of children to laugh at, and be scared by, the same kinds of things. It is the quality of the exploration of relationships, rather than a specific philosophy, that makes this book one of the best among adolescent fiction.

As for *Nobody's Family is Going to Change*, both this and our other suggestion for a class reader which should be in every school's stock, *The Friends* by Rosa Guy, were first recommended by friends outside teaching who had an interest in children's fiction. Their descriptions of these books were of particular interest since we were looking to introduce more multi-racial literature into a school without one black face, where feelings of ignorance and prejudice can run high. This can only be done if the literature is of sufficient quality; a good intention alone is not sufficient to warrant taking the racial debate into the classroom. If we intend to challenge received views we cannot do that through threadbare literature. We would recommend certain books for private reading, such as Jan Needle's *My Mate Shofiq*, which we would not use as a class reader. Consciousness of its condescension has now overtaken the teacher's favourite *The Cay* by Theodore Taylor – and not before time. We are now having to find new books by writers such as Mildred Taylor, Rosa Guy, Julius Lester and Louise Fitzhugh to recommend to our classes.

Nobody's Family is Going to Change is special because it deals primarily from within the black family, developing an empathy most children respond to, rather than a sense of injustice children are supposed to feel against prejudice and racism. Not that racial injustice is swept under the carpet. We see its effect upon the children's father, whose lifelong struggle as a second-class citizen has left him bitter and authoritarian. In trying to make sure his children escape the indignities he has suffered, he is in danger of denying the individual wishes and talents of Willie, a natural dancer, and of Emma, who is a serious, intelligent student. During the novel we come to see the struggle between father and children from both sides, even if most of the children's sympathies lie fairly and squarely with Emma and Willie during their conflict with their father. Here is an example of Emma's musing in serious vein which illustrates the intensity of family hostility in this book:

I'm facing that I'm a loser. What more can I do? *Why* bit into her brain like a small spider. Why am I a loser? She sat very still. Because it pleases my father. The thought flooded over her. She felt relief, a horrible kind of relief, but relief nevertheless. She thought again of her father looking like a rock . . . a huge boulder, a mountainous expanse of rock settled into the land, never moving.

It is this book which will provide the basis for the half-term plan of work that will be described in the concluding section of this chapter. For the present we propose to consider some tactics that the teacher might use, to ensure personal engagement in class reading.

Living the Novel

As pupils it is likely that many of us suffered the classroom reader as a wholly boring experience. The obligatory reading of passages aloud from ill-suited classics, with comprehension questions at the end of every chapter to test memory rather than understanding is a sure way to ruin most literature. If we were lucky we might have also experienced the class novel read well and presented by a teacher who believed in sharing the novel communally; but if we did 'live the novel' as pupils, it was probably through our own private receptivity rather than through techniques of presentation.

To make the most of the actual process of reading the novel to the class the teacher needs to be rehearsed for this just as much as for any other English activity; reading aloud may appear less demanding than running a class discussion but it is surely no less important. At the risk of stating the obvious the teacher's task is to make sense of the words on the page through emphasis and variation of tone, and to make the text come alive with the same kind of intensity we would demand from an actor reading a script. A way of including the class in the process of reading, while avoiding tedious monotone readings, is to give out character parts to those children willing and able to read aloud – thereby leaving the teacher to read the narrative and some character parts. It will probably be necessary for those pupils to rehearse their reading if it is to carry dramatic credibility. Every teacher knows about the success of virtually every 'play-reading' in the classroom – providing the teacher keeps it tightly organised; without detracting from the style of the novel, this dramatic element increases the value of the novel as a shared experience. Admittedly, this technique cannot be used with every novel, where it is not always clear who is meant to be speaking; but wherever possible we would encourage teachers to try this method out, even if it means some time is spent working out speaking roles or line allocations in difficult passages. This may sound too much like turning the novel into a play script; but provided the integrity of the novel is maintained it draws children into active participation with the book.

During the reading there is the thorny problem of whether to interrupt the flow of the narrative with questions and observations, or whether to leave these until the end of the chapter. On the whole, classes who enjoy the class novel will complain if any interruption is made. It is up to the teacher's judgement whether this is due to idle minds or a genuine desire to get on and find out what happens next. It is also up to the teacher's judgement when and if to question pupils on their understanding and interpretation. Usually we find it is best not to interrupt unless there is a natural pause in the story, or unless there is a genuine problem of understanding character motivation or plot structure. At the end of chapters well into the book you might be fortunate enough to experience the spontaneous, natural and excited discussion about the characters or the story's development, so that all your carefully planned open-ended questions become redundant.

Where possible the teacher should exploit the spontaneous desire in younger children to relate the novel to their own experience. Anecdotal discussion is worthwhile if it helps participants to understand the book. Sometimes this will have to be on their own terms. At its simplest an example might be taken from *Carrie's War*; when we are first introduced to Samuel Evans and his poor sister the over-powering atmosphere in their house is of extreme order and cleanliness – leading in the context of this story to a grim godliness. Many children have extremely house-proud relations who have at some time caused embarrassment, irritation or amusement. Similarly, the moral dilemmas posed at a deeper level in many novels will need first to be understood in terms of their personal experience by many young readers. If the teacher can help to manoeuvre children into a synthesis between the book and their 'reality', their level of involvement will have deepened. However it needs to be said that if the book remains entirely on the pupils' own terms, unmediated by those viewpoints to which the teacher can alert the reader, the child's perceptions are likely to remain shallow.

What about the follow-up work and work around the novel in progress? This is a vital part of enabling the child to live the novel in a creative way. But it must not be over-done; it is unnecessary to dwell on every chapter or important event. Whether the activity chosen by the teacher is dramatic discussion or writing it should ensure that pupils absorb the book into their own thinking. Otherwise it will be seen as something merely external to themselves.

How then do we strike the right balance between enabling opportunities for personal response and over-doing follow-up activities at the book's expense? There is no simple answer here, although there are considerations such as the length of the book; how well the book lends itself to creative departures; and, ultimately, the readiness of the class to respond to the book. As we shall show in the half-term's outline, some activities ought to be suitable for the whole class, whether designated 'mixed ability' or not. But experience shows that some element of choice often produces the most valuable responses. A word of warning: it is unwise to extend any work too far beyond the time spent actually reading it. Furthermore, the reading should be concentrated; while the class novel is the main component of English work in progress as much time as possible should be given over to it each week. Once a week for a single or double lesson is not enough – the longer the period of time the reading takes, the more diluted the impression and response. As to length, we consider that some editing is necessary with almost every book. Teachers should expect to edit (but not censor) rather than see editing as an admission of failure; to enjoy an apple you do not need to eat the pips. Neither should we expect every child to read at the same pace. The shared experience is valuable at first, but the most engaged and independent readers may become frustrated and want to go on faster. Rather than holding them back the teacher might allow them some private reading after they have read a section of the book with the class.

What about projects? Some teachers will find that the enthusiasm generated by some classes for a particular book will lead naturally into some kind of extended work. For example, after reading *Grinny* it might seem the right moment for a short project on space monsters, aliens, or science fiction. By all means take advantage of such a chance if it is offered; but have clear guidelines, for children's interest can prove fickle without the book's regular stimulus.

Drama, though often still restricted by lack of facilities, should be seen as a necessary extension and vehicle for absorbing the novel. By drama we do not mean simply acting the section of the book just read. There may be a place for this, but on the whole the response is usually shallow and uninventive. Such acting out seems most worthwhile if done for the fun and entertainment value (see the lesson plan for 2 October, page 84). A drama lesson might involve taking a scene from the book and widening its scope; at its most elementary, perhaps, it can be an acting out of the kind of anecdotal discussion mentioned earlier. Or it may be a dramatic prediction of what happens next; or putting the book's characters into situations only implied, thereby giving a different perspective on the plot, or motives. These last two methods will often allow pupils to show comprehension of a kind they would find hard to write down. Perhaps teachers will want to use drama first and foremost to examine the novel's concepts. Something as hard to handle as sexism can be handled more easily in drama generally, when pupils act out their own experiences; when they do this for characters in a book there is often a deeper understanding of the book's meaning and intentions (see the lesson plan for 25 September, page 83). Drama can also be considered as a useful means to introduce the next section of scenes or cluster of ideas in a novel. Potentially difficult or boring passages can be made more accessible or enjoyable by using drama beforehand – rather than, as is the usual practice, afterwards. (We have used this approach with some success, to inspire interest in selected classroom library books as well.)

For those who lack confidence in teaching drama, the classroom reader can provide a welcome base and structure, a touchstone for the teacher and a stimulus for children who are being asked for a more exploratory response than may be possible within the usual patterns of

English work. There is no inherent reason why the English classroom should not also be the site for drama – we would at least encourage those who are hesitant to try some gradual transitions of this kind. If successful, it can be one of the most stimulating experiences to teacher and taught; when the class reader is supporting and informing dramatic work, there are enhanced opportunities to develop a sense of discipline in drama.

Apart from drama there needs to be a variety of interesting and relevant written activities which allow for the class to broaden their involvement in, and enjoyment of, the novel as they grow into understanding. We should not expect children to write merely for the sake of writing, and there is no need for the class to produce a set ration of written work automatically each week. If writing is not felt to be personally motivated it loses virtually all value.

Nor should the teacher expect the class to listen to the book for too long at any one time. In a long lesson, while preserving the continuity of reading, the teacher needs to be armed with activities appropriate to whatever stage the book has reached. Common sense suggests that a lesson need not begin with reading; for example, it is a good idea to play the psychological game from *The Pigman* that Mr Pignati plays on John and Lorraine before reading this chapter. Perhaps this is a gimmick, but it brings the class into the novel by another route; and in the weeks taken to read any book, variety has its uses.

When the novel is under way it is useful to establish clearly the characters involved, their different personalities, how they inter-react, and any background information which will clarify the book for those members of the class whose enjoyment, in the early stages particularly, will depend upon such basic comprehension. The confidence and involvement of the whole class can be helped along at this stage by setting the same 'open-ended' task for all children, thus encouraging a common purpose, and also allowing a wide range of response. For example, after the first two chapters of *The Midnight Fox* the class might be asked to identify with Tom, miserable because he is going to stay with relations, by writing about a time when they were in similar circumstances. After the first two chapters of *Carrie's War* we might ask second year pupils to write Carrie's and Nick's diaries relating to the early events in the book. This kind of written role-play should begin to alert the class to the sharp differences between Carrie's and Nick's view of what is happening. Also, as preparation for the first drama lesson connected with *Carrie's War*, intended to explore evacuation, some of the class can be set to preparing evacuees' labels, while the others write letters to the local headmistress (like characters in the book) accepting at least one evacuee and stating a preference for either a boy or a girl. This kind of written work, advocated by Dorothy Heathcote (1980), who frequently uses letters, official documents and newspaper articles to underpin her drama, brings an authenticity to drama and integrates written activities into other patterns of work.

By the third year 'identifying' with characters is perhaps not sufficient; we might now expect children to show a deeper understanding of character and motivation, and be able to write a detailed character sketch using details gleaned from the text. In order to facilitate this children might be asked to compile ideas and perceptions about characters in different columns or boxes which are to be filled in at certain stages of the reading. Some pupils will be able to do this while they are listening to a reading, others will need time set aside afterwards with teacher guidance. By this method the class steadily builds up a more detailed picture of characters. Their early, often inadequate impressions are augmented or replaced by a more complex understanding as the novelist enlarges the portrait. This approach allows them to see clearly in black and white terms how their own understanding develops, as the novelist releases more information into the narrative. Often some kind of diagram can be used to show the relationships between characters; a visual representation often clears up confusions which would otherwise hamper the kind of basic comprehension so essential to the less able reader's enjoyment. A clock helps many children to follow the events in Billy Casper's day; a cartoon can help them understand the use of flashbacks in Billy's mind; a map may be a handy mental peg on which to hang a number of ideas.

Further into the reading, when interest has been generated and characters live more boldly in the imagination, children will be able to follow an individual interest. Ideal for allowing this kind of wide choice is a task sheet to fill in with information about a particular character, a map outline requiring details, or a small diary to be written as if by one of the characters in the book. The worksheets should have a variety of activities suitable for a range of abilities; ideally they should be colour-coded, to be easily stored and recognised. In *The Midnight Fox* the range of ideas to imitate and personalise include 'Amazing Headlines', 'Food Inventions', 'Questionnaires', 'TV Show Scripts', and 'Time Capsules'. From *The Pigman*, 'Telephone Marathons', 'Problem Page', and newspaper reports are just some of the many activities thrown up by events in the book. There are many possible openings for stories and/or playscripts about teenage problems; parties; arguments between parents and teenagers; boy-girl relationships. The book also invites some writing of scenes from points of view other than those of the character narrating that particular chapter; Lorraine and John are constantly cross-questioning one another's version of events, but what is Mr Pignati's? These tasks vary in their general appeal – some may need to be compulsory, others strictly a matter of individual choice. Activities planned should allow for a balance between private and group work, and for different kinds of discussion and writing. None of these suggestions should be taken as a list of tasks to be invariantly applied, since any work of fiction will present its own individual possibilities. When the reader chooses a book he or she also chooses which parts to read intensively, which passages to skip, whether or not to re-read, and so on. Thus as private readers we choose our own approach to the book. The class reader removes an element of this choice; but, where possible, activities planned to accompany a book should try to restore some of this free choice, and make allowances for those pupils who will want to see the book as 'fun', while encouraging a deeper response through some more strenuous demands.

We also need to encourage pupils to examine the text in greater detail in order to understand the reason for changes in tone, point of view, and why styles are appropriate to different moods and intentions. The best kind of comprehension activity (we use 'comprehension' here in its broadest sense) is one where the reader is made to 'look between the lines', inferring the complexities of the author's intentions as well as absorbing the style. At least half-way through reading class novels cloze passages might be prepared occasionally from a part of the book already read. The most rewarding approach here seems to be taking out key descriptive words, rather than mechanically every fifth or seventh word. There is a danger with younger readers that cloze passages will be seen as memory tests or a rushed guessing game with scores out of twenty. This can be resisted by pair or group work, ideally ending with a class discussion where choices are explained and justified, as with 'I think it's shrill because she's used that word about the fox's bark a lot of times.' When checked against the original version, the chosen words should be discussed for quality rather than marked simply right or wrong.

Another useful comprehension activity is 'prediction'. When a book is going well it is possible to invite spoken and written prediction of the book's development, which will show the teacher the extent to which the pupil is understanding the characters and their thinking, within the mental constructs set up by the novel. The teacher can choose an appropriately exciting or important moment to spark off this kind of activity, once the class is far enough into the book to know enough about the characters, also perhaps, to feel enough about them to value this kind of work. A set sentence or short paragraph to continue from serves as useful guidance to those children who will find this kind of thing difficult. Prediction is not an easy thing to do, but most children can gain some benefit; most pupils can produce interesting ideas, although they may not all be able to develop these ideas or express them in the book's style as well as the best in the class.

Finally, when the book is finished there is useful work to be done in retrospect – surveying the overall structure and development. Books like Van der Loeff's *Children on the Oregon Trail* or *Run For Your Life* by David Line beg to be plotted as maps; books with a central important relationship which fluctuates distinctly can be plotted by line graphs with chapters along the horizontal and the degree of friendliness/ hostility plotted on the vertical (ideal for Rosa Guy's *The Friends*). Such visual representation will not invariably be helpful; if teachers feel that this simplifies, rather than elucidates, then it is inappropriate. Yet it can serve often as a useful rounding off of the work; or, if used during the reading, as a thread for many to hang on to during the several weeks of reading.

A Half-term's Plan of Work

Nobody's Family is Going to Change by Louise Fitzhugh was chosen for a mixed ability third year group, in a deliberate attempt to use good quality multi-racial fiction as a natural part of the variety of children's literature. *Nobody's Family* portrays a black, middle-class professional American family, and could be criticised for its apparent wholesale adoption of white ideals and aspirations; but is sufficient treatment of what it means to be black in a white culture to acquit the book of this complaint. The exploration of injustices and misunderstandings is subtle yet accessible to young readers, and much of the book's attraction comes from the very immediate, domestic nature of the problems. It can be found in the classroom that children identify with these problems primarily because they have grown out of the theme of children controlled by adults; thus the empathy with characters that reading encourages can both transcend and – at the same time – unite cultural differences.

Despite the unique, almost eccentric qualities of the main child characters, Emma and Willie Sheridan, their predicament inspired identification in all but one third year pupil, a boy with reading difficulties who admitted he couldn't really understand what was going on, let alone empathise with characters. The main character, Emma Sheridan, is a fat, black, budding feminist. Her brother Willie is a complete contrast – a small boy whose only thought is how to follow his uncle on to the stage as a tap dancer. Gradually their cause – the struggle of children to be taken into account by their parents – gains strong sympathy from the reader; and the children's capacity for survival and liveliness won over those sceptics in the class who were disapproving of the 'serious' theme.

Every timetabled English lesson (with the exception of one private reading lesson a week) was used for reading or working on the book. A choice of activities for any follow-up work was usually offered – for example, either a playscript or a more reflective personal piece of writing. There was also a timetabled drama lesson every week devoted to extension of ideas in the book; here again an element of choice was offered. Extracts from the teacher's notes on these lessons are given below:

9 September
Read for forty minutes, introducing Willie's obsession with dancing, the beginning of Emma's struggle to convince her father that she can and will become a lawyer like him – or at least be considered suitable for such 'male' professions. It was noted that she has a tendency to withdraw into a lively inner life.

Choice of written work:
1   A playscript in which they were to put themselves on trial for something they shouldn't have done, perhaps cheating or starting a fight without cause. These ideas come directly from the first of Emma's many

internalised courtroom dramas where she tortures herself (satirically) for having eaten too many cream horns at lunch.

2   (Intended for more reflective writers.) A description of the relationship between a brother and sister, with particular reference to changes and developments over several years. Here is the conclusion of one girl's attempt at this:

> When me and my brother were younger we used to get on better than we do now. When Darren was a baby I used to play with him and make him laugh. As he got older we started to argue and blame each other for things we got into trouble for. He is now ten and I'm thirteen and we never agree.
>
> *Dawn*

11 September

A forty-minute drama lesson. Some groups chose to act out their mock trial scenes written in the last lesson; others tried out a scene which would prepare them for the battles Emma would fight later in her struggle for independence. In pairs the children were given separate briefings:

A   PARENTS: You want your child to work in a bank like father. You are waiting up till eleven o'clock one night for him/her to return home. You are worried and annoyed.

B   TEENAGERS: You have just formed a pop group with some friends. You have been at a rehearsal for your first public performance tomorrow night. You are frightened to tell your parents because you know they wouldn't approve. You return home at 11 o'clock to find one of your parents waiting up for you.

14 September

Read on, witnessing Emma's violent dislike for her brother's dancing obsession; her self-disgust; and the beginnings of her crusade to persuade her father that she is intelligent and suitable for a profession, particularly his own. At this point, thirty or so pages into the book, the class were asked for the first time whether they were enjoying it, and the response was overwhelmingly enthusiastic.

16 September

Read on to page 50. Emma in despair of her father's attitude happens to see a TV programme which seems to offer answers to her problems – a child's organisation dedicated, to all intents and purposes, to fellowship and self-help. Meanwhile Willie truants from school to visit his uncle for a forbidden dancing lesson. A choice of written work was offered at the end of the reading:

1   Continue the story of what Emma discovers about the organisation known as 'The Children's Army' beginning with the sentence, 'When school let out, Emma ran to the delicatessen at the corner.' (She goes to buy cookies which are the entrance fee for the meeting of the Children's Army.)

2   In pairs draft the Children's Charter Emma was trying to write before she discovered the existence of the children's organisation. It should be a list of beliefs in the form of a manifesto.

The class found both of these activities difficult, but they are both worth plenty of discussion and class preparation time.

18 September
Forty-minute drama lesson, using an edited section on Emma's visit to the Children's Army Convention, to explore without necessarily imitating the text. The 'cases' of three children were read out, who needed the organisation's help against oppressive or brutal parents. The class chose which of these three 'commissions' they would work on in groups of three or four. Interestingly, the results were similar to Emma's conclusions in the book.

21 September
Showed ITV programme from 'Making a Living' series which concerned two girls employed in traditionally male jobs. Class were asked to write a summary of what the women had said, and, relate this to Emma's experience. Here are two short extracts from pupils' work:

> The girls were doing men's work and must have had a lot of guts to work with men in this way. The programme links with *Nobody's Family* because Emma wants to be a lawyer, which according to her father is a man's job.
>
> *Paul*

> The girls in the programme were very much like Emma because they are both determined to do the job they want to.
>
> *Elizabeth*

23 September
Read on. Another meal-time scene in which Willie is finally banned from dancing and, for the first time, Emma openly sides with her brother against her father.

25 September
Forty-minute drama lesson. Used the ITV programme as the source for two short improvisations. The first, in pairs, was a Careers Officer faced with a client wanting information about a job normally considered for the opposite sex. The second was a scene in a pub between a group of friends, one of whom has a job considered unconventional for their sex.

28 September
Read on. Emma meets with a group of girls from the Children's Army to swop stories of parental injustice. After careful consideration, Emma decides to take up Willie's case in earnest.

30 September
Continued the reading. Willie disobeys his father and earns a part in a Broadway musical. His mother begins to take his side in a flush of maternal pride. The written work set was another of the problems Emma poses herself. She tries to devise a questionnaire to expose how adult attitudes are harmful to children. Having produced her questionnaire, Elizabeth went on to diagnose scores in the following manner:

5–10   You are obviously concerned about what happens to your children.
25–30 You are quite a strict parent. Your children need a bit more freedom . . .

Several children asked their parents to fill in the questionnaires, and Carol's mother commented, 'Interesting subject for thirteen year old.'

2 October
Drama. For fun, class auditions were given for a Miscellaneous Musical Extravaganza. The success of this may be an indication of how much the class had enjoyed reading about Willie's audition.

5 October
Finished reading the book. Mr Sheridan morosely resigns himself to his children's determination and Emma forms an alternative to The Children's Army composed of girls who will help each other to fight conditioning and family pressures to accept stereotyped sex roles. The class said they would have preferred an epilogue to the ending, so that they knew what eventually happened to Willie and Emma.

7 October
Surveyed the class opinions and objections. All but three pupils said they had enjoyed the book and would recommend it to others of their age. Most liked Willie best and enjoyed those sections in which he figured most. Many admitted they had found Emma's internal musings difficult to follow. Everyone said they had enjoyed the drama connected with the book; almost everyone had enjoyed and gained benefit from the questionnaire; many admitted they had found the Children's Charter difficult. Most claimed they had learnt more about the problems of sex stereotyping, including Karen who said: 'I have learnt that girls in boys' jobs is not so bad after all,' and Michael who said: 'Well, I think girls can be in boys' jobs. Why not? It sounds good.'

Finally, the class found that Emma's family was, to their obvious surprise and pleasure 'just like mine'. The questions put to the class were rather blunt, and even optimistic responses are only crude indicators of a book's value, but the answers confirmed that *Nobody's Family is Going to Change* provided the material for a highly successful sequence of lessons, where enjoyment was not sacrified to educational intentions, and where some of the most pressing social problems of our time were approached via personal and domestic contexts understandable to most children.

Bibliography

(i) General

DEPARTMENT OF EDUCATION AND SCIENCE (1975) *A Language for Life* (The Bullock Report) (HMSO)
HARDING, D. W. (1937) 'The Role of the Onlooker', in *Scrutiny* VI (3
HEATHCOTE, D. (1980) *Drama in Context* (NATE)

(ii) Children's Books

ASHLEY, B. *The Trouble with Donovan Croft* (Penguin/Puffin)
BARSTOW, S. *Joby* (Heinemann/New Windmill)
BAWDEN, N. *Carrie's War* (Penguin/Puffin)
BYARS, B. *The Midnight Fox* (Penguin/Puffin)

BYARS, B. *The Eighteenth Emergency* (Penguin/Puffin)
DAVIES, A. *Conrad's War* (Hippo)
FISK, N. *Grinny* (Penguin/Puffin)
FITZHUGH, L. *Nobody's Family is Going to Change* (Armada/Lions)
GARNER, A. *The Owl Service* (Armada/Lions)
GUY, R. *The Friends* (Penguin/Puffin)
HINES, B. *A Kestrel for a Knave* (Penguin/Puffin)
HINTON, S. E. *The Outsiders* (Armada/Lions)
LAYTON, G. *Northern Childhood: The Balaclava Story* (Longman)
LINE, D. *Run for your Life* (Penguin/Puffin)
NEEDLE, J. *My Mate Shofiq* (Armada/Lions)
O'BRIEN, R. *Mrs Frisby and the Rats of NIMH* (Penguin/Puffin)
ROBINSON, B. *The Worst Kids in the World* (Hamlyn/Beaver)
TAYLOR, T. *The Cay* (Penguin/Puffin)
TOWNSEND, J. R. *Noah's Castle* (Penguin/Puffin)
VAN DER LOEFF, A. R. *Children on the Oregon Trail* (Penguin/Puffin)
WESTALL, R. *The Machine Gunners* (Penguin/Puffin)
ZINDEL, P. *The Pigman* (Armada/Lions)

NOTE   As most editions suggested are paperback reprints, dates of first
publication have not been given.

6 Poetry in the Secondary School: The Divining of Words

Bernard T. Harrison

From the thought the remembrance,
From the remembrance the consciousness, the desire,
The Word became fruitful . . .

from 'Cosmogony', Maori Chant

In the old Maori chant it is held, as in diverse cultures throughout the world, that the divine *Word* conceives and brings forth all creation, all meaning. The power of mankind to generate meaning through the living breath of the speaker is called poetic power. In many cultures poets have been granted a special, even holy status as seers, prophets, revealers of truth concerning the past, the present and the future. Obversely their words have been misunderstood, or reviled as seditious, or mocked as the products of madness – as with Blake, or Shelley. There is Shakespeare's self-confession that lunatic, lover and poet are of imagination all compact:

> The poet's eye, in a fine frenzy rolling,
> Doth glance from heaven to earth, from earth to heaven;
> And as imagination bodies forth
> The forms of things unknown, the poet's pen
> Turns them to shapes and gives to airy nothing
> A local habitation and a name.
>
> *A Midsummer Night's Dream*

Poets in our own age are praised and publicised; they are also neglected or condemned for being boring or effete, or needlessly obscure; or perhaps even worse, they may be condescended to as hack entertainers, or as pedlars of easy-serve propaganda, so that the trite and the fake come to be taken to represent the best the poetry can do. In the face of so many extravagant claims both for and against poetry, is it surprising that we should wonder sometimes whether poetry stands much chance in secondary schools? Are we ourselves close enough to poetry to present its attractions? As listeners or as readers, and as teachers, do we dare to confront its dangers?

Given the utilitarian drive behind much of our secondary schooling, that question is bound to be put out of a sense of dismay, from time to time. As English teachers we have all read and listened to claims made about the primary importance of poetry in the classroom. Yes, we may agree, it would be pleasant to agree with Tolstoy's view that art need not – indeed, ought not – be elitist; and that 'good art always pleases everyone'. By all means let poetry be for the people, and let the people be for poetry. But then, whispers the cynic within us, Tolstoy did not have to teach the class of unruly fourteen year olds from that city housing estate last term. And even given a thriving English department and a school which has learned to value books and plays and other art activity, how many of us would declare that the choosing and presenting of poetry involves no special difficulties – that it is as easy, say, as choosing and presenting fiction to all our English classes? How many of today's inspectors and advisers and Heads of Department can concur with HMI Temple's Report (1881–2) that 'I have been the ardent champion of this subject (poetry) for many years, and am very glad to say that in my district it is almost universally taught, and in the great majority of schools taught well'?

Of course, our notions of what is meant by 'taught well' are now thoroughly altered. With hindsight gained after a hundred years of practice, we may be more likely to doubt whether poetry has ever been taught as well as it deserves – whether, even, it ought to be taught as such, at all. In particular most teachers would now reject with vehemence the Victorian Inspectors' requirement that classes should learn whole passages of 'classic' poetry by heart. But setting aside questions of method for the moment, we have to ask ourselves whether we still believe now, along with HMI Temple and his colleagues of a hundred years ago, in the worth of poetry, and in its place in schools. As an article of faith, on which the rest of my case depends, I should nail this thesis to my chapter: that the study of poetry ought to be the very heart of English studies. Yet it is not easy to defend this view with the same whole-hearted simplicity of spirit as HMI Temple. Victorian enthusiasm may now seem like overstatement. A Ulysses-like wariness may be called for, if the case for poetry is to be accepted: for we live now in a world which no longer needs to pay even lip-service to the claims of poetry. Even so, we still come occasionally across a statement about the overwhelming importance of the *quality* of language, which carries something of the old power to compel a respectful – even fearful – assent. We can recognise, for example, just what it is that George Steiner is predicting, when he declares that

> . . . unless we can restore to the words in our newspapers, laws, and
> political acts some measure of clarity and stringency of meaning, our lives
> will draw yet nearer to chaos . . . 'To perish by silence': that civilisation on
> which Apollo looks no more shall not long endure.
>
> *Language and Silence*, 1969

A poet's lucidity will never be wholly Apollonic, but it is a poet's first task to identify, to give a 'local habitation and name' to things. It would be a poor poet who had no concern for 'clarity and stringency' of meaning, nor for the truths that poetic art directs itself to seek out. Poetry is, at best, the most distilled art-truth. It is the essence on which the language of newspapers, laws and politics must draw for their clarity. It contains more important powers for human survival than we usually dare to acknowledge.

As far as English teaching in general is concerned, it would be of interest if we could ascertain, even in crude terms of hours and percentages, just how much poetry is studied in our secondary schools. No one knows the whole picture, although one local survey (by H. Gordon, 1981) has investigated the time devoted to poetry study in all the English lessons (including Sixth Form groups) throughout the secondary school of a 'Northtown' Local Education Authority (LEA), during one whole week near the middle of the Autumn term. The survey revealed that only about one tenth of all the time allocated to English studies was spent on poetry study; and assuming that English lessons usually comprise something like one seventh or one eight of the whole timetable for most secondary school students, this would indicate that no more than 1.5 per cent of a school student's time each week is likely to be spent on the study of poetry, in that particular LEA at least (the survey excluded five schools which were contacted but which refused or failed to make returns). Unsurprisingly, schools varied considerably in their individual provision of poetry lessons, ranging from none to half of all the English time available. The survey found (again, unsurprisingly) that teachers who read and enjoy poetry themselves are far more likely to present poetry to their classes. If the overall dismal findings of this survey are at all representative of the present state of poetry teaching in our schools, two urgent general points need highlighting: first, that a good deal more poetry ought to be presented in schools; and second, that given all the pressures from the rest of the curriculum, we should take unusual care to ensure that poetry is taught well, so that it may be enjoyed by, and may carry value and meaning for our students.

For a start, it might prove useful if members of an English Department agreed to use part of their next departmental meeting to consult together and admit briefly to each other their own present attitudes to poetry. This may well reveal unexpected positions, as it did among a group of teachers at a recent NATE Conference on Poetry Teaching. Yet such attitudes, once admitted, can swiftly be transcended, through advice and support from colleagues, and through self-reflection. Several members of the group confessed, for instance, that the prospect of teaching poetry caused them anxiety, because they felt uncertain even about how and where to look for suitable poems, let alone how to teach them. Another declared that after abandoning her PhD research project to become a teacher, she felt herself still to be too involved in escaping from the straight-jacket of 'Eng. Lit.', to approach poetry teaching with any sense of freedom and enjoyment (this was in total contrast to my own confessed feelings of relief and victory, whenever a poetry/fiction/drama element can be inflitrated through the constraints of 'Language' courses in an Education Department). Other contributors dwelled on the need for more attention to performance aspects of poetry, in order to gain a sense of poetry as lived experience; on the limiting, even damaging effects of public examinations on poetry teaching; on the limitations of anthologies, and so on. Eventually we identified twelve propositions, or questions, which covered some key aspects of choosing and presenting poetry in the classroom. Six of these focused on choosing, and six on presenting poetry.

Choosing

1 *What poems should we choose, in order to give pleasure?*

It has long been respectable in theory to acknowledge a 'pleasure' principle in ordinary school class work, although this may be less often conceded in practice. Yet poetry teachers know that more than in any other area of English teaching except drama perhaps, the teacher depends on the willing, unembarrassed engagement of the class for a successful lesson. The presence of a spirit of play, and the notion of poetry study as an enjoyable, absorbing game, tend to decline as learners advance through the school system. We need to ask what choices of poetry, if any, can reverse this process, to restore a sense of fun, even delight, in the experience of a poem. Most obviously, pleasure can be gained through a simple relaxing of usual seriousness and decorum; frivolity and knock-about humour have their place in poetry, as in life. For many children and adults their idea of 'fun' poetry may not have extended beyond Spike Milligan and Pam Ayres (or the lightest products of Betjeman, as an 'up-market' option). Teachers would not be hard-pressed to add Lewis Carroll's nonsense poems, together with limericks, jingles and parodies from the several collections of nonsense poetry now in print, and from other sources such as television and journals. Such nonsense and 'honest vulgarity' have always been the staple diet of children, as the Opies' *The Lore and Language of Schoolchildren* (1959) has charted. These traditions have long held their place in popular taste, mainly through ballads and the music hall; and recent years have seen a windfall of such verse by writers who have often been closely associated with schools. Michael Rosen, for instance, claims that poets are 'comedians, teachers, smarty pants, show-offs, nags, hecklers, gassers, frauds, actors, conjurers, mimics, orators, conversationalists, thinkers' (*I See a Voice*, 1981, published along with a popular Thames Television series of poetry programmes for schools). This breezy, anti-posh (urban, not urbane) view of poetry colours the work of such writers as Adrian Mitchell, Roger McGough and Michael Rosen himself, all of whom have been personally involved with schools' poetry, through performing and talking and teaching and workshop visits. *I See a Voice* will doubtless win wide attention from English teachers. It is playful and unstuffy, and seeks also to extend its readers into areas of poetry beyond the jokes and nonsense of the early pages. Some of the poems with a 'social message' are crude in their one dimensional propaganda. But the main aim of this book is to show how poetry, including thought-provoking poetry, can give pleasure; and this aim is quite well achieved in many of the choices and suggestions for further activity. It is an aim which all teachers of poetry would do well to keep in mind.

2   Is there a body of 'children's poetry' as there is of 'children's fiction'?

A view is now emerging, that the study of children's poetry has been neglected in schools, at the expense of children's fiction. Yet it is doubtful whether children's poetry as a genre can be identified anything like as clearly as children's fiction. A useful initial attempt to collate sources of poetry written especially for children has been made by Michael Benton ('Poetry for Children', 1982); but there is obviously far greater overlap between children's and adults' interests in poetry, than in fiction. Teachers may work with profit from Dr Benton's select list of ten nineteenth-century and twenty twentieth-century writers, but even for the primary school they will also wish to add many other poems from past and present writers. They need, of course, to pay careful heed to the needs of particular age and attainment-groups, but a wide range and variety of choice are essential for all classes; inflexible categorising is not likely to be helpful, since so much depends on the poetic experience, the quality of relations, and the whole cultural climate of a particular classroom. While John Donne would never be chosen for twelve-year-olds, it is also true to say that they need not be restricted to a diet of nonsense-and-narrative. Young children can show remarkable understanding of qualities of feeling and tone in a ballad like 'The Unquiet Grave', or Wordsworth's 'Lucy' poems. In seeking out appropriate poems for children, we are bound to respect their levels of sophistication and areas of interest; but there is no evidence that children *feel* experiences less complexly than adults. Sensitive choices of poems can contribute much towards the young readers' verbal realising of experiences, actual and imagined. On the whole all poetry which is truly 'simple, sensuous and passionate' is likely to have value for children, as much as for adults.

3   Is it best to keep to modern English poetry?

As has been seen, the notion of a special category for 'children's' poetry is not altogether helpful; nor, where children are concerned, is the almost opposite notion of 'classical' poetry. We are now far removed from the days when children were expected to memorise and recite a hundred lines from Shakespeare or Milton or Tennyson, in order to satisfy a visiting Inspector. We may indeed have come full circle, in that teachers are now tempted to follow the modern fashion of drawing exclusively on the work of living British poets, since this poetry seems likely to be most 'accessible' for today's classes. Can this be justified?

The short answer must be no. While it is understandable that much of the poetry presented in schools prior to 16+ and 18+ examinations should come in this category, this provides no good reason for a general 'rule'. A great living abundance of past poetry and of overseas poetry will be neglected, and we should be diminished unless we seek it out. Such poetry may present extra difficulties to inexperienced readers but can extend vastly their sense of time and place. Traditional songs and ballads (of course), Shakespeare's songs, Saxon and medieval poems in modern form (for example, the splendid Exeter Book riddles translated by Michael Alexander in *The Earliest English Verse*; Alexander's translation of *Beowulf*; Ian Serrailler's translation of the *Sir Gawain* legend), Herbert, Cowper, Blake, Wordsworth, Clare, Coleridge, Hopkins, Edward Lear and Hilaire Belloc all come to mind, among obvious choices from the living past. In fact it can be a fascinating and enjoyable discipline, to restrict choices for a class to pre-1900 poems for, say, half a term, in order to investigate the many possibilities among earlier poems. Selection needs to be judicious and sensitive to the experience of the class; but on grounds merely of accessibility, there is much to choose from.

There still remains a gold-mine, virtually unexploited in many classes, which contains all those poems written beyond the British Isles, yet within the English-speaking tradition. West Indian, Australian, American, African and Asian sources, both present and past, yield many splendid poems. America's Emily Dickinson and Nigeria's Wole Soyinka are just two of several poets of the first rank, who deserve study as individual makers, as well as winning their place among the most popular school anthologies. West Indian writers like Edward Brathwaite and Derek Walcott provide access to a refreshing cultural tradition which has now moved much nearer to our own, through the cross-cultural infusions of immigration and of modern communication patterns. Such extensions of English-speaking literary traditions should be welcomed and exploited for the enrichment of our poetry classes.

Nor should poetry in translation be neglected. The heritage of so many groups and cultures are now made available in collections such as Willard Trask's *The Unwritten Song* (1969). Here can be found Creation myths, songs of birth, war, love, childbearing, feuds and death; tales of family life, of hauntings, of animals; celebrations of the seasons, of the universe, of the spirit of place. Then there are individual writers such as Yevtushenko (USSR), Rabindranath Tagore (India), Lao Tzu (Ancient China) or Miroslav Holub (Czechoslovakia) – these and many others are available in inexpensive paperbacks. And there is, of course, the Bible, as well as the Holy works of other religions – the *Bhagavadgita*, the Koran, the Sacred Songs of the Navajo, and many others. All of these should be within our range of choice, to extend awareness of the infinite richness and flexibility of poetic metaphor.

4   *Should poetry be serious, as well as enjoyable?*

Reflecting on his own poetry, Christopher Logue has said, 'Whatever poetry I write has got to be quite good, otherwise there's no point. There's thousands of years of good, light entertaining poetry; no need to add more to it' (*The Times*, 21 November 1981). We can see what he means when we look at many recent school anthologies; and it will soon be realised by our students that deeper levels of enjoyment depend eventually on the inherent seriousness of the poem, and on the seriousness of the reader's involvement. An exclusive diet of nonsense and limericks would be eventually as tedious as Christmas games that go on too long. Of course, to be serious need not mean to be over-earnest or solemn, it does not exclude joy, frivolity, nor verbal equivalents of Charlie Chaplin. To be serious is not to imply that *all* our chosen poems are to be on War, or Peace or topical issues such as community or sex relations (though these and other 'serious' issues will be unavoidably aired in any good range of poetry). But it does imply that we are guided inevitably by a concern for the *quality* of poems, even though our standards of choice may well shift from time to time. In choosing poetry for the classroom, 'anything' will *not* do. We seek poems which will disturb consciences, awake yearnings, provoke us to laughter in spite of ourselves, evoke passionate agreement and disagreement, refresh imagination. Above all, we seek poems which will remove the smudges of past imprints from our vision, which will coerce us into first-hand response. On one occasion the right choice might be Herbert's 'Redemption'; on another, Soyinka's 'Fulani Creation Story'; or on another, Elizabeth Jennings' 'Rembrandt's Late Self-Portraits'. Whatever the choice the aim will always be to remove accretions of old dust from our vision. Seriousness, then, resides in a *quality of attention*, rather than in any particular gravity of tone; it is a capacity to endow all events, however slight, with import. Consider, for instance, the marvellous, visionary attention of Emily Dickinson's 'A Bird came down the Walk' (1862):

> A Bird came down the Walk –
> He did not know I saw –
> He bit an Angleworm in halves
> And ate the fellow, raw,
>
> And then he drank a Dew
> From a convenient Grass –
> And then hopped sideways to the Wall
> To let a Beetle pass –
>
> He glanced with rapid eyes
> That hurried all around –
> They looked like frightened Beads, I thought –
> He stirred his Velvet Head

Like one in danger, Cautious
I offered him a Crumb
And he unrolled his feathers
And rowed him softer home –

Than Oars divide the Ocean
Too silver for a seam –
Or butterflies, off Banks of Noon
Leap, plashless as they swim.

Here, even (or one might say, especially) the punctuation is perfectly concentrated on the wonderful singularity of this bird's behaviour. It is a quality of interest which is more than self-conscious, more than scientific; the poem reveals a perfect subjectivity of contemplation, in that it is the poet's experience of the bird which makes the event important, or 'serious'. In the words of one of our pupils, 'The seriousness of a poem is its sincerity, the way a poet's feelings become apparent. That is not to say that a poem should be without humour' (Lisa, aged 14). Through such a sincerity of attention comes the unfolding of original feeling, of new meaning on behalf of the future. For the poet, the study of a bird's activity is, like the future itself, a serious business.

5 Should poetry be 'taught'?

In his book *The Poetic Achievement of Ezra Pound* (1979) Michael Alexander reflects on the advent, with Pound, Yeats and Eliot, of the 'difficult' poem which came as a refreshing antidote to the intellectual pap of so much Victorian verse. But a less happy growth from the impact of 'difficult' poetry, Alexander suggests, is the cult in our century of the 'teachable' poem, whereby only poems that can be analysed for their strenuous language or meaning are thought to deserve academic attention. The error has spread to schools, and remains embedded in 'Eng. Lit.' examining patterns; but all teachers who have an ounce of respect for poetry will know there are many poems which we would murder to dissect, yet which have the strongest claims for inclusion in the classroom. We need not always choose our poems with a view to 'comprehension' or other kinds of work, spoken or written. Since the sole end of introducing poetry into the classroom is to engage the sincere attention of the children, there must be provision for the kind of response that is by no means easily definable – 'Blow, Blow thou winter wind . . .' 'Summer is icumen in . . .' 'Should auld acquaintance be forgot . . .' 'She dwelt among the untrodden ways . . .' 'There were two sisters in a bour . . .' 'I am black, but comely, O ye daughters of Jerusalem . . .'

Such poems (and this may be true for a great number of poems) cannot be 'taught', in the usual sense; they can only be read, heard, shared, pondered on and performed, and read again (though it would be foolish deliberately to inhibit natural conversational dialogue in a classroom on any poem). The teacher's ingenuity will still be taxed well enough when direct teaching is dropped, if proper attention is given to the sense of occasion and quality of performance in the classroom. To choose 'unteachable' poems is not to evade 'difficulty' in the poetry class; on the contrary, it is to acknowledge that difficulty can only be confronted through personal engagement, and that this is sometimes best achieved without another's intervention. Without response there can be no ordering of response, no matter how impatient the teacher may wax. Once a degree of personal connection has been gained on the student's terms, then there may be intervention and extension of access through the teacher – but not, by any means, with each and every poem that is introduced to a class. Forced feeding may produce rich examinees' livers, but at the cost of an impoverished experience of poetry.

6   *How far should we rely on anthologies?*

During seminars at the conference a number of teachers admitted their dissatisfaction with poetry anthologies. Individual anthologies can range from good to abysmal, of course; but even the best are, by their very nature, piecemeal. Nor can this problem be put right by the 'thematic' anthologies that have proliferated in recent years, where poems of often quite disparate quality and interest are yoked together under some unlikely connecting theme (a passage from 'The Ancient Mariner', Edwin Muir's 'The Combat', Nissim Ezekiel's 'Night of the Scorpion' and so on, all under a heading of 'Travel and Adventure'). While anthologies – even 'thematic' anthologies – can provide valuable classroom resources, they ought not to be used exclusively. It is worthwhile to ensure that in any year with a particular class, a few individual poets are given more substantial attention, in order to develop a sense of the poet as a maker of a body of poems. There are many possibilities: for the first/second year, Rosen, Roethke, Brown-john, Belloc, Lao Tzu, Carroll, Brian Jones, Hardy, border ballads, Causley, Hughes, Sandburg, de la Mare, MacBeth, Eliot's *Old Possum's Book of Practical Cats* (1939), D. H. Lawrence, Emily Dickinson, Eleanor Farjeon, and so on. For the third/fourth year, Soyinka, Larkin, Heaney, Frost, Hughes (again), Stevie Smith, Thwaite, R. S. Thomas, Blake, Wordsworth, Brock, Browning, Chaucer, Shakespeare, Auden, Yev-tushenko, Lawrence (again), Scannell, the Psalm-writers, and many, many more. Moreover, teachers themselves need to be active antholo-gisers, not merely depending on the judgements made in published anthologies; and they ought in turn to encourage their students to compile personal anthologies of favourite and important poems. Yet while anthologies should not be used exclusively there are many that deserve warm recommendation; for example *The Rattle Bag* (1982), compiled by Seamus Heaney and Ted Hughes, offers many delightful and original extensions to the usual diet of classroom poetry.

Presenting

7 What kinds of advance planning are needed, to ensure good variety of presenting?

This question has to be faced well before the teaching year begins, so that the most obvious method (which can work perfectly well, on occasions) of handing out a poem, reading it out and then asking questions, does not become an inescapable rut for teacher and class alike. Having shared the task of seeking out new sources of poetry, the English department should now look at the layout of classrooms, as a first step in planning for varied modes of presentation. Are poetry books available in the classroom – in class libraries, in small sets – for children to browse among and make their own choices? Are there wall displays of poems and poets – linked possibly with pictures, with topics, with news items? Is the room suitable for choral and/or musical activity, and can space be made or found for dramatic and dance performance? Can furniture be arranged conveniently for small group discussion? Are there enough supplies of scissors, paste, pencils, paint and brushes for personal anthologies and poem-poster work (or can working links be made with the art department here?). Are a tape recorder, record player, radio, television and a slide projector available, to aid different kinds of performance? Can the department arrange to invite a poet into the school, to talk to and work with poetry classes (Regional Arts Associations can help here)?

Such collaborative advance planning would be guided by a view of poetry that acknowledges its links, as an oral and literary art, with the visual, aural, plastic and kinetic arts. It is likely that many departments might feel they would benefit from outside consultation on these issues – with colleagues from other schools, with advisers and inspectors, and through in-service courses. If this is so, a clamour ought to be made locally for consultations and for courses, since many voices will be needed to win recognition for refreshed attitudes to poetry study. Meanwhile, some initial ideas might be drawn from a book such as Michael and Peter Benton's *Poetry Workshop* (1975). See also the useful article 'Thirty-six Things to do with a Poem' (*Times Educational Supplement*, 20 February 1981) by Geoff Fox, Brian Merrick and other contributors from a NATE group on poetry teaching.

8 How should poetry be performed?

The fact that poetry has roots in oral traditions should alert us to seek out the potent energy of these traditions through performance. As with fiction by far the most important influence here, of course, will be the teacher's own capacity to read aloud well. This needs careful rehearsal; for instance, most student-teachers need to learn the art of really slow, deliberate reading which makes full use of pauses and silences; or how to draw out the rhythms of a poem; or how to exploit shifts of movement, contrasts of mood and dramatic elements in a poem.

Furthermore the teacher who can play a musical instrument, or who is willing to sing (and most people have a good enough voice to render, say, a border ballad like 'The Twa Corbies' effectively, given practice) starts with a great advantage in the poetry class.

But the teacher's reading/performance is only one mode; and more than with fiction perhaps, the class should be usually involved. 'I have often found,' declares Lisa, 'that a poem in front of me has more effect on me when different people read it, not just the teacher.' This is especially so if there are speaking parts in a poem. Pupils can be set to prepare readings of a poem in pairs or groups (say, different poems by the same writer, or a group of poems which illuminate or contrast with each other) for presenting to the class, or for a taped 'radio' presentation. Or the class can work together at a choral performance of, say, Brian Stone's robust translation of the Medieval 'Blacksmiths' poem, with full sound effects; a great range of poetry is available here, and whole anthologies have been devoted to choral work. Ballads and rhythmic chants are specially suited to this treatment. See for instance J. C. Gibson's and R. Wilson's *Solo and Chorus* (1964) and R. Finnegan's *A World Treasury of Oral Poetry* (1978).

Poems such as Soyinka's 'Fulani Creation Story' or Blake's 'Poison Tree' can be well rendered through mime and dance; other poems can be linked effectively with slides and photographs (Elizabeth Jennings' 'Rembrandt's Late Self-Portraits' is an obvious example here). And not least, poets can be given a chance – on record, through the media, as visitors – to present their own poems. Who, for instance, can read Seamus Heaney's poetry better than the poet himself?

9   What questions should be put, and how?

Given that poetry has first to be communicated and has to be experienced before a more focal understanding can be achieved, how should we move forward then towards more formal exploration, when the occasion demands? If the presentation/performance has been at all successful, the initial stages of questioning need tactful handling. Responses to the poem may still remain at a very provisional, tentative stage; questions need to offer a willingness to remain faithful to whatever small, vulnerable impulses of inner emotional living have been quickened, in first encounters with the poem. Sometimes it is best to wait a while for someone in the class to put the first question, rather than offer some clumsy space-filler like 'Did you enjoy that, then?' or 'Do you like snakes/lions/acrobats/rabbits and so on?' After reading William Stafford's 'Travelling through the Dark' with a third year 'mixed ability' class, a boy whose own reading and writing record had been very weak over several years interrupted the pause after a reading of the poem with the compelling question 'Couldn't he cut it out?' He referred to the driver's dilemma, on finding a deer stiff and cold in death by the roadside, whose belly is yet warm with a living foetus. The boy's question was prompted by the most genuine involvement in the events of the poem and the feeling of the poet. If it was naïvely put, it also directed the class immediately to what Matthew Arnold termed the 'central, the truly interesting' elements of the poem; and the teacher on this occasion hardly needed his carefully prepared set of questions, which were designed to move the class through an account of the details of what happened, to wider reflections on the metaphorical weight of the dead deer and the 'living' car beside it. (See Bernadette Walsh's account of her work on poetry with 'remedial' classes, for further evidence of children's capacities for self-initiated creative response.)

When given the chance, pupils can often be depended on to put the questions of closest concern to themselves. Of course the teacher can refine and extend these; but it is important to set tasks that are within reach of pupils, and can be pursued as an interesting game. Rather than dwelling always on formal questions of meaning, for instance, it can be a good idea to require a class to select the most important sentence or phrase(s) in a poem, or to underline the six (or more, or less) most important words. Titles, last verses, final lines of each verse can be removed, and the class asked to give their own version. 'Predicting' tactics can be used, where the first verse of, say, Philip Hobsbaum's 'The Place's Fault' (about being bullied at school) is given, and the class speculate on how the poem might develop before being given the rest of the poem. Cloze procedures, too, can be useful in moderation. All these tactics are directed to engaging the class in closer textual attention, through setting a sense of 'problem'.

10 What further activities are possible?

If, say, it has been decided to give some special attention to poetry over half a term of English lessons, it might be of interest to conduct a 'before' and 'after' survey of class attitudes to poetry ('Can you name five poets?' 'Do you have a favourite poem/poet?' 'Do you think a poem should have to rhyme?' 'Do you read poetry by choice, for pleasure?' 'Can you quote one/two/three/four lines of poetry? If so, show in the space below . . .' and so on). 'Before' and 'after' results might then be collated, compared and discussed. Another way (recommended by the 'Thirty-six Things' group) of concluding a series of poetry lessons might be to arrange a 'Desert Island Poems' programme in small groups with a tape recorder, to present favourite poems with readings and reasons given for selection.

Some poems lead quite naturally to other, extra-poetic activity. Alan Brownjohn's 'Common Sense', for instance, is compiled from a 1917 textbook of common-sense arithmetic; the social/historical information that is thrown up unconsciously by the extracts from the book and put in ironic light by Brownjohn will need comment beyond the poem itself. Similarly, poems such as Soyinka's 'Telephone Conversation', Heaney's 'Whatever you do, say nothing', Peter Porter's 'Your Attention Please' or Mary Horton's 'Spectators' can hardly be left just as poems: it would be as wrong to dodge the political and social criticism contained in these poems, as to commit the opposite error of 'filleting' literature (to use a term from the Bullock Report) merely for its sociological interest. Poems with political, social and moral bite demand of us that the issues they point to should be scrutinised, as well as the poetic statement; the English teacher has a duty here to seek out further information and comment. (Malcolm Stanton's chapter 'Towards Public Issues' shows the kind of commitment that is possible here.)

One opportunity for further work, learning poems by heart, is now out of favour. Yet anyone who visits an Old People's Home may discern how those who once had to learn verses by heart can find great pleasure as adults in repeating their 'favourite' poems. Of course, a requirement to learn by heart should not be pressed to the point of dreariness or punishment. But as a preparation for a performance, or for an exchange of recitations in small groups, it can be a valuable, enjoyable activity, which implants words that may be savoured into adult life.

11   *How should we teach the formal terms?*

Diction, syntax, rhythm, assonance, imagery, tone, rhyme, scanning . . . herded together like so much ill-assorted gymnastic apparatus, the formal terms that we use to describe the poetry must be off-putting. It is little wonder that rather than risk losing their pupils' goodwill when engaging with poetry, many teachers choose to avoid mention of the terms altogether, until the demands of public examinations coerce attention to them.

Yet the real features of poetry that the terms point to cannot be decently ignored, if there is to be any kind of considered exploration of a poem. The phrasing, the rhythm, the tones and the metaphorical substance of a poem are its very body; and if we work the right way round (from the poem that is, not from a shopping list of terms) we can hardly help but attend to them. Rhythm, of course, will be experienced through performance, and should enable students to recognise the supple range of ordinary speech rhythms, from which good poetry always draws:

> Absent thee from felicity a while,
> And in this harsh world draw thy breath in pain,
> To tell my story.
>
> *(Hamlet)*

Given any attention to the movement of the lines here, how can the speaker avoid taking a breath at 'draw'? And rhyme should be experienced as it is in nursery rhymes: a kind of magic circle, holding a thought or feeling in perfect, charmed captivity:

> Who said 'All time's delight
> Hath she for narrow bed,
> Life's troubled bubble broken'?
> That's what I said.
> (de la Mare, 'Song of the Mad Prince')

Inexperienced pupils will only feel dismay at any direct requirement to discuss 'phrasing', 'diction' or 'tone'; yet they can work quite capably at particular tasks which will draw them towards handling these terms ('How do you think we should say this phrase aloud?' 'What words and phrases belong together in this verse?'). As for imagery, this is one term that cannot be evaded, being the very centre of poetic expression. A good way of introducing the term ('simile', 'metaphor' and 'symbolism' can come later, if required) is to find a poem where the images are drawn from the whole range of sense experience – touch, smell, hearing, taste, vision – in order to show how the term draws on *all* imagining activity, not just visual 'images'. Useful choices might include R. S. Thomas' 'Poetry for Supper', or (obviously) Seamus Heaney's 'Death of a Naturalist', or 'The Pond' by the West Indian poet Mervyn Morris:

> . . . And in its depths, old people said,
> swam galliwasps and nameless horrors;
> bright boys kept away . . .

In this poem, the boy's imagination is in fact 'demystified' when he goes himself to look in the pond, and 'shimmering in guilt,/he saw his own face peering from the pool'. The poem shows well how visual evidence is only one part of our whole imaginative life.

12 *How should we encourage pupils' own writing of poetry?*

The question cannot be answered here; it demands another chapter. Clearly there will be many overlaps between pupils' response to poetry, their writing on poetry, and the writing of their own poetry. I have dwelled on how pupils can respond to and participate in poetry rather than on how they themselves may become makers of poems. Yet once the pattern of reading and enjoying poetry is achieved, there is no doubt that the one activity will enhance the other. The poetic achievements of children at all stages of schooling are now well documented in the many anthologies of children's writing available, and in many excellent class and school magazines that circulate at local levels.

If the poetry class has been successful, it may be that any writing on poetry will be highly involved and personal, demanding extra tact from the teacher (or other audience). Given the opportunity, writing on poetry can quite often become writing *in* poetry; and the act of writing a poem is likely to be the most private, personal undertaking of a pupil's whole classroom experience. The good teacher will tread softly here, though this need not mean a wholesale withdrawal of critical interest. Pupils can be given considerable help in the process of emotional clarifying (see, for example, the account of a poetry class in David Holbrook's *English for Meaning*, 1979), and also in coping with particular poetic forms (see Sandy Brownjohn's *Does It Have to Rhyme?*, 1980). While poetry lessons need not and should not end always with a writing task, it can be claimed that a successful poetry lesson provides possibly the best of all possible groundworks for good personal writing.

The final words of this chapter should go to a poet. In 'Rembrandt's Late Self-Portraits' Elizabeth Jennings pays tribute to Rembrandt's creative vitality and courage in words which may extend to all art, including poetry itself:

> To paint's to breathe,
> And all the darknesses are dared. You chose
> What each must reckon with.

References

ALEXANDER, M. (1979) *The Poetic Achievement of Ezra Pound* (Faber)

BENTON, M. (1982) 'Poetry for Children' in *Children, Language and Literature* (Open University Press)

FOX, G. and MERRICK, B. 'Thirty-six Things to do with a Poem' *Times Educational Supplement*, 20 February 1981

GORDON, H. (1981) 'The Status of Poetry and its Role in the Secondary Curriculum', unpublished MA thesis (University of Sheffield)

Further Reading

1   While study of individual poets is recommended, there are not many whole volumes by individual poets that are obviously suitable for younger classes. Penguin, Faber and other lists can be consulted, and the following should be useful:

BROWNJOHN, A. (1970) *Brownjohn's Beasts* (Macmillan)

CAUSLEY, C. (1975) *Collected Poems, 1951–75* (Macmillan)

BLAKE, W. *Songs of Innocence and Experience* (Penguin)

BELLOC, H. *Selected Cautionary Verses* (Penguin)

HUGHES, T. (1963) *The Earth Owl* (Faber)

HUGHES, T. (1976) *Season Songs* (Faber)

DE LA MARE, W. *Collected Rhymes and Verses* (Faber, 1970)

SCANNELL, V. (1972) *After the Apple Raid and other Poems* (Chatto)

2   The following collections and anthologies are recommended:

ALEXANDER, M. (ed.) (1977) *The Earliest English Poems* (Penguin)

ALEXANDER, M. (trans.) (1973) *Beowulf* (Penguin)

ASTON, A. (ed.) (1977) *Poets in School* (Harrap)

BENTON, M. and P. (1969–71) *Touchstones 1–5* (Hodder and Stoughton)

BENTON, M. and P. (1975) *Poetry Workshop* (Hodder and Stoughton)

BENTON, M. and P. (1979–82) *Watchwords 1–3* (Hodder and Stoughton)

BERNIKOW, L. (ed.) (1979) *The World Split Open: Women's Poems 1552–1950* (Women's Press)

BLACK, E. L. (ed.) (1966) *Nine Modern Poets* (Macmillan)

BOOTH, M. (ed.) (1981) *Contemporary British and North American Verse* (Oxford University Press)

ENRIGHT, D. J. (ed.) (1980) *The Oxford Book of Contemporary Verse* (Oxford University Press)

FIGUEROA, J. (ed.) (1982) *Caribbean Voices* (Evans)

FINN, F. E. S. (ed.) (1976) *Here and Human* (Murray)

FINNEGAN, R. (ed.) (1978) *Penguin Book of Oral Poetry* (Allen Lane)

GIBSON, J. (ed.) (1973) *Let the Poet Choose* (Harrap)

GIBSON, J. G. and WILSON, R. (eds.) (1975) *Poetry Pack* Sets 1 and 2 (Macmillan)

GIBSON, J. G. and WILSON, R. (1964) *Solo and Chorus* (Macmillan)

HARRISON, M. and STUART-CLARK, C. (eds) (1981) *Narrative Poems* (Oxford University Press)

HARRISON, M and STUART-CLARK, C. (eds) (1980) *Poems*, Volumes 1 & 2 (Oxford University Press)

HEANEY, S. and HUGHES, T. (eds) (1982) *The Rattle Bag* (Faber)

HEWETT, R. P. (ed.) (1978) *A Choice of Poets* (Harrap)

HIDDEN, N. and HOLLINS, A. (eds) (1978) *Many People, Many Voices* (Hutchinson)

MACBETH, G. (ed.) (1980) *Poetry 1900 to 1975* (Longman)

MCGOUGH, R. and ROSEN, M. (1981) *You Tell Me* (Penguin)

OPIE, I and OPIE, P. (eds) (1973) *The Oxford Book of Children's Verse* (Oxford University Press)

PALMER, R. (ed.) (1980) *Everyman's Book of British Ballads* (Dent)

PARSONS, I. (ed.) (1979) *Men Who March Away* (Heinemann)

ROSEN, M. (1981) *I See a Voice* (Hutchinson)

SERRAILLER, I. (1981) *The Challenge of the Green Knight* (Penguin)

STONE, B. (ed.) (1970) *Medieval English Verse* (Penguin)

SUMMERFIELD, G. (ed.) (1970) *Voices* Books 1 and 2 and *Junior Voices* (Penguin)

THOMPSON, D. (1978) *Distant Voices: Poetry of the Preliterate* (Heinemann)

TOWNSEND, J. R. (ed.) (1973) *Modern Poetry* (Oxford University Press)

TRASK, W. R. (ed.) (1969) *The Unwritten Song* (2 Volumes) (Cape)

WAIN, J. (ed.) (1979) *Anthology of Contemporary Poetry* (Hutchinson)

WILSON, D. G. (ed.) (1975) *New Ships* (Oxford University Press)

WOLLMAN, M. (ed.) (1975) *Ten Twentieth Century Poets* (Harrap)

WOOLGER, D. and OGUNGBESAN, K. (eds) (1978) *Rhymes and Rhythms* (Oxford University Press)

3 Poetry Response and Poetry Teaching:

BROWNJOHN, S. (1980) *Does it Have to Rhyme?* (Hodder and Stoughton)

BROWNJOHN, S. (1982) *What Rhymes with 'Secret'?* (Hodder and Stoughton)

DANBY, J. (1940) *Approach to Poetry* (Heinemann)

English in Education Journal (NATE Publication), various articles on poetry teaching.

FINNEGAN, R. H. (1977) *Oral Poetry* (Cambridge University Press)

HARRISON, B. T. (1979) *Poetry and The Language of Feeling* (Tract No. 27, Gryphon Press)

HOLBROOK, D. (1979) *English for Meaning* (NFER)

HUGHES, T. (1967) *Poetry in the Making* (Faber)
OPIE, I. and P. (1959) *The Lore and Language of Schoolchildren* (Oxford University Press)
REEVES, J. (1965) *Understanding Poetry* (Heinemann)
THOMPSON, D. (1978) *The Uses of Poetry* (Cambridge University Press)
Use of English Journal, various articles on poetry teaching.

4   Some Addresses:

Argo Records, Decca Record Co., 113–115 Fulham Road, London SW3 6RR
Arts Council Poetry Library, 9 Long Acre, London, WC2 9LH
Arvon Poetry Foundation, Lumb Bank, Hebden Bridge, W. Yorks, HX7 6DF
BBC Publications and Broadcasts, The Langham, Portland Place, London W1A 1AA
NATE, 49, Broomgrove Road, Sheffield, S1O 2NA
Poetry Society, National Poetry Centre, 21 Earls Court Square, London SW5
Regional Arts Associations For addresses, write to Hon. Sec., Standing Conference of Regional Arts Associations, 31, New Bridge Street, Newcastle-on-Tyne, NE1 8JY
Use of English Journal, Scottish Academic Press, 33, Montgomery Street, Edinburgh EH7 5JX

7 Fiction for the Fourth Year: Enabling Personal Bearings

David Allen

Teachers search endlessly for the class reader that 'works' in the fourth year; for the novel that engages and pleases the very disparate interests, and that matches the very different reading levels within any normal class of pupils of that age. When the group is of mixed ability, deliberately so chosen, the task of finding one book to please everyone becomes downright impossible. This does not necessarily mean that the class reader is a non-starter, only that it is of limited scope. There are few novels that will do the job; those few should be used sparingly and with due attention to the best way of avoiding constrictive lock-step while savouring a shared reading. (By lock-step I mean holding all children to the same uniform reading pace.) Most of the time devoted to reading in the fourth year should seek to reflect the wide range of interests, aptitudes and capacities of the students, rather than pretend to a unity that rarely exists.

I am not thinking here of a formal literature course with an examination in sight; such a course demands special approaches because of the odd requirements of memory that are required. However, I would contend that the kind of work that I shall outline provides a good foundation for any formal study because it seeks to encourage *reading* (many pupils take literature exams with too little acquaintance with books and so cannot make comparisons) and the asking of *questions*. Yet it might be said that reading is a kind of interrogation; the skill depends on asking the most fruitful kind of questions. It is in this sense that the farmer or sailor 'reads' clouds, or that we 'read' a face.

Asking Questions

Too often reading in the classroom follows the pattern of teacher choosing task, teacher guides pace of reading, pupils answer questions about the text chosen by the teacher. The apparent purpose behind this activity is to transmit a way of reading, things to look for, points to clarify. However, as Christopher Walker has pointed out with younger children (in *Reading Development and Extension*, 1974) this does not really teach children to read actively, *interrogatively*, for that is a concern that antecedes reading. While open-mindedness is to be respected, this ought not to imply blankness in the learner. We want to give space to the personal, enquiring presence of children, who can approach reading with a purpose, a set, a cluster, of questions in mind. It is worth reminding ourselves how we fluent, committed readers come to a book. We come with a whole bundle of expectations about the nature of a book (humour, mystery, realism), about the author, about what is likely to be expected of us. We also have, based on wide reading, a set of tastes and preferences – of topic and content, of style, even of length of chapter and paragraph. This whole set of expectations enables us, even when we think we are reading the book open-mindedly word by word, to select and pattern the meaning that comes to us. One of the questions we work on in reading novels is, 'Is the life in the novel like the life that I know?' Another is, 'Is it understandable in the light of the life I know?' We might call a book that seems to be describing existence as we know it 'realistic', 'convincing', even 'true'. Conversely, few of us can continue to read with enjoyment a book that would appear to be attempting to be 'realistic' when we feel that it fails to do so.

Of course many novels are not purporting to be about recognisable life, and in any case I set aside the whole problem of whether a novel of any kind can be said to be about 'real' life. Nevertheless I contend that my reading is not untypical, in that I demand from novels some convincing parallels with the world I observe outside the world of literature. The reading approach that I shall describe seeks to have students framing questions of this kind before they come to a book. The questions are generated by discussion, drama, even by some selective dipping into some of the books that will form the central activity.

Making Choices

Schools do not build in much choice for their students even in English lessons. Choice is often seen as dangerous, as indeed it is, for choice brings the possibility of mistakes. Yet choice is an absolutely crucial part of learning; its absence castrates the power of learning. I am not just taking a 'liberal democratic' position here, though it is clear that a sense of responsibility requires a choice to have been made; and if schools prepare our children for a liberal democracy we should be trying to encourage the civic virtues of deliberation, responsibility and taking an interest. None of these can develop if the child is allowed no say, no effective say in what he or she does.

However, as Margaret Donaldson has argued in *Children's Minds* (1978) the reasons for choice are rooted deeply in what we understand of the whole process of learning and of thinking. Certainly reading is honeycombed with choices if it is to be real interaction between reader and text rather than just a skim across the surface.

Margaret Donaldson makes two points in particular that are of far-reaching importance and which this approach to literature attempts to embody. She is considering the way we need to stand back and look at what we are doing if we are best to carry our task through. She writes, 'If a child is going to control and direct his own thinking . . . he must become conscious of it.' To this end she recommends that we get children to talk about their own actions, so that they are more aware, for

> . . . awareness typically develops when something gives us pause and when consequently, instead of just acting, we stop to consider the possibilities of acting which are before us. The claim is that we heighten our awareness of what is actual by considering what is possible. We are conscious also of what we do *not* do – of what we might have done. The notion of *choice* is thus central.

The implications of these remarks are very far-reaching. Much of schooling restricts choice, allows little contemplation of alternatives. Yet if she is right, as I believe she is, then the curriculum is absurd if it does not attempt to act upon this underlying principle. What I suggest attempts at least over eight to ten weeks to construct a way of working on literature that embodies the principle. Before going into detail, it is necessary to give an outline sketch.

The teacher draws together as many novels as possible which seek to describe and explore the contemporary world of the older adolescent or the early stages of adulthood. These are made available in the classroom for extensive and intensive reading after preliminary work and discussion, reading of extracts and drama improvisation, to set up a number of general questions which are to be answered by the reading. During the weeks of this work the pupils are asked to keep notes in the form of a journal and to report back to the class from time to time what they are up to and what their thoughts are at present. Alongside the reading time the pupils are asked to undertake a piece of writing themselves which explores their concerns or the concerns revealed in their reading. This writing may take the form of a story, a series of poems, or an expanded reflective journal. The culmination of this work is to choose the five novels that in the opinion of the class reflect contemporary life in a convincing way, and to 'present' in some way part of a novel that interests them.

This bald outline misses out the complexity of the preparation and the give and take during the lessons. Whether the whole enterprise is a charade or not depends on very careful teaching in the early stages so that real questions emerge that are of real interest to the pupils. Of course to have a curiosity about people like oneself is very natural; literature draws on and stimulates that curiosity.

The Books and the Introductory Stage

There have been many books published recently which seek to mirror the world of the late teenager and the young adult. A catalogue of their recurrent themes would seem to draw a problem-laden picture of that stage of development, so much so that many have criticised some writers for stressing the problems. Nevertheless, students in the fourth year of secondary school are, typically, encountering abiding questions of identity, personality, relationships with the opposite sex and with older people, questions about the kind of society we should like to see. Literature offers a deep fund of examples, fragments of lives lived like our own, yet not like our own. During the reading course that I am outlining, a wide range of books is made available to the class, so that they may choose, read, and reflect on what they read. The books are selected from as many sources as the teacher can find: stock, library loan, begged or borrowed, so that there develops a *problem* of choice. Initiative in bringing together a good stock of books was always needed; it is certainly needed in these more parsimonious times. The list I suggest here is far from exhaustive and can be added to at any time during the course. You can compile your own. Hardback publishers are shown in square brackets.

STAN BARSTOW, *The Human Element*, Longman (Imprint Books).

HAL BORLAND, *When the Legends Die*, Penguin (Puffin Books).

VERA and BILL CLEAVER, *Dust of the Earth*, [Oxford University Press].

VERA and BILL CLEAVER, *Trial Valley*, [Oxford University Press].

FARRUKH DHONDY, *Come to Mecca*, [Collins] Armada (Lions).

FARRUKH DHONDY, *The Siege of Babylon*, Macmillan.

MARGARET DRABBLE, *The Millstone*, [Weidenfeld and Nicolson] Penguin (Peacock Books).

JANE GARDAM, *The Summer After the Funeral*, [Hamish Hamilton] Penguin (Puffin Books).

ROSA GUY, *The Friends*, [Gollancz] Penguin (Puffin Books).

BARRY HINES, *Looks and Smiles*, [Michael Joseph].

NIGEL HINTON, *Collision Course*, [Oxford University Press] Penguin (Puffin Books).

LINDA HOY, *Your Friend, Rebecca*, Bodley Head.

JOHN KNOWLES, *A Separate Peace*, Heinemann (New Windmill).

JULIUS LESTER, *Basketball Game*, Penguin (Puffin Plus).

JOAN LINGARD, *The Clearance*, [Hamish Hamilton] Heinemann (New Windmill)/Hamlyn (Beaver Books).

JOAN LINGARD, *Hostages to Fortune*, [Hamish Hamilton] Penguin (Puffin Plus).

JOAN LINGARD, *A Proper Place*, [Hamish Hamilton] Penguin (Puffin Plus).

LOIS LOWRY, *A Summer to Die*, [Kestrel] Mayflower (Dragon Books).

MICHAEL MARLAND (ed.), *Loves, Hopes and Fears*, Longman (Imprint Books).

K. M. PEYTON, *Flambards Trilogy* (*Flambards, The Edge of the Cloud, Flambards in Summer*), [Oxford University Press] Penguin (Puffin Plus).

K. M. PEYTON, *Pennington's Heir*, [Oxford University Press] Methuen (Magnet Books).

BARRY POINTON, *Cave*, [Bodley Head].

DAVID STOREY, *Saville*, [Cape] Penguin.

J. R. TOWNSEND, *Goodnight, Prof, Love*, [Oxford University Press] Heinemann (New Windmill).

VARIOUS AUTHORS, *Our Lives*, ILEA English Centre.
PAUL ZINDEL, *I Never Loved Your Mind*, [Macmillan] Armada (Lions).
PAUL ZINDEL, *My Darling, My Hamburger*, [Bodley Head] Macmillan.
PAUL ZINDEL, *Pardon Me, You're Stepping on My Eyeball*, [Bodley Head]
   Macmillan/Armada (Lions).

I have not tried to select only books of quality, since one of the aims of
the reading is to encounter different levels of quality. However, I have
not included books which are in my opinion wholly meretricious (and
there are many of those in the 'young adult' category). Some students
will also read *Jane Eyre*, or *Call of the Wild*, or *Sons and Lovers*. Where
possible the books should be held together in the same place for the
duration of the work so that the students may change them whenever
convenient. It is no part of the scheme to make it difficult to borrow
books. Some will want to read many of the titles; others will want to cut
their losses with a book that is going badly and to get their hands quickly
on a replacement.
   Once the books are collected the first stage is to set the central
discussion in motion and to introduce a handful of the books as tasks
and testers. I suggest the following five make good starters: they set up
a sense of rich possibilities and alternatives: *Looks and Smiles*, Barry Hines;
Your Friend, Rebecca, Linda Hoy; *The Seige of Babylon*, Farrukh Dhondy;
Pennington's Heir, K. M. Peyton; *Saville*, David Storey.
   A part of each book is chosen by the teacher to be read aloud and
discussed. The aim here is to arouse interest in the question of whether
the writer is dealing with a recognisable world. The extract from Hines'
novel, *Looks and Smiles* (pages 10–24 in the hardback edition), is long
enough to give something of the variety of events, yet keeps the thread.
Mick has just left school and the novel recounts his unsuccessful
attempts to find a job. The section chosen describes Mick's brush with
the police and his visit to the Careers Office. The discussion usually
starts with a fairly superficial exchange of generalities such as, 'It was
like that when . . .' and 'That reminds me of when . . .' These attempts
to relate the events of the novel to events in everyday life are too easily
suppressed by an impatient effort to move matters on to more rigor-
ous 'lit. crit.' (which too often means telling pupils what to think). It
is the character of the work I am describing that such attempts to relate
to one's own biography should be accepted and developed. Only when
the comparisons are sufficiently extensive should the teacher focus
discussion back on to the Hines novel. Here there are a number of spots
to look at carefully. Mick has responses to 'authority', in the form of his
father, the Careers Officer or the policeman, which are worth
discussion and which are sensitively characteristic of people of his age.
The question should arise as to why Hines chose to write about the
careers interview. However, there may be other aspects of the reading
that the class would like to pursue. Follow where the class wants to go.
   The underlying thread remains the same throughout: is the writer
handling a world I recognise? The next four extracts (from the other

novels selected) present strong contrasts with the Hines novel. As each one is read and discussed, the central question becomes more complex, more articulate, and the class recognise that there are different views of 'reality', in fiction and among their fellows. They should also become more aware that a writer selects from an infinite list of alternatives.

To provide an interesting contrast, *The Siege of Babylon* by Farukh Dhondy, whose writings remind us of the multi-cultural nature of our society, presents images that some of our students find exotic, puzzling, mysterious. Others find his writing threatening. Yet others find his world appealing, speaking for them. This novel is an interesting example of his work. It is in some ways a 'cops and robbers story' but with a range of complex attitudes on the part of the writer as to who if anybody is in the right, the group of young black men who attempt a robbery, fail and then are penned down under seige, or the whites, liberals, radicals or reactionaries.

The extract to introduce here is the opening chapter, in which the siege has already started. (The novel consists of a number of moves back in time to explain how it all came about.) The challenge of this first chapter, following on from the Hines novel, is that the world is both very different, yet also recognisably similar.

For example, authority is again an issue. However, after exploring these connections (and any other aspects that are found of interest) the main thrust of the discussion should be to consider the role of the image of the siege, obviously deliberately selected by the writer to sum up the relationship of the black community to the white. There are obvious parallels to be drawn with the careers interview in Hines' novel, and the question is likely to arise as to whether Hines and Dhondy are distorting reality in their selection. The question need not be settled, nor need the idea of propaganda be explicitly raised. These are areas that can be followed through more thoroughly at a later date. The purpose here is to explore the writer's choices, for these perceptions are to be employed in the student's own writing.

As each of the introductory excerpts are read and discussed, the match between the novel and apprehended reality is further explored. *Your Friend, Rebecca,* by Linda Hoy is a perceptive treatment of an unhappy adolescent, told with a wry authentic humour. There is an accessibility about the experience being handled, a vigour in the detail. *Pennington's Heir* by K. M. Peyton (or an alternative, *The Millstone* by Margaret Drabble) again presents a contrast of background, for Pennington is a talented classical pianist, doted on with a passion by Ruth in a way some readers may feel entirely convincing yet objectionable. Is the relationship one of female subservience to male self-absorption and if so should the writer deal with it so apparently approvingly?

A danger in this kind of comparison is that only large issues and broad themes are discussed whereas, of course, it is in the tissue and texture of the words that the life of a piece of writing resides. Much of the discussion around the central question of 'a convincing world' will naturally focus on this word and that phrase, should do so indeed; and if necessary the teacher should gently encourage a savouring of the language of the extracts, a tasting of the 'resonance' of the words, the power of complex associations.

In this kind of enquiry, the teacher brings a very important viewpoint – someone who has been able to look back on that stage of life. The reading, the exchanges, all begin to take on a wider perspective if such a viewpoint is given its place. I have chosen *Saville* by David Storey (a very fine novel indeed) to represent the adolescence I knew. The texture of this novel is so very different from life today that a look at it throws into relief much that seems muddled because we are too close to it. The novel serves as a touchstone throughout the reading. Some will read the whole book. At several times over the weeks further extracts will be read aloud as the students' writings, dramatic presentations, taped readings are presented to the group for reflection.

Immersion in Reading and Writing

After the initial readings and discussion, during which the central questions are agreed, the class moves on to immersion in reading. The first stage, the discussion of extracts, takes about a week. The next stage, the reading, will occupy the next several weeks. During that time the main thrust is to get a substantial amount read and pondered on in the light of the questions. While the reading is going on, the teacher will discuss quietly with each individual or group what they are up to.

It is important that this work takes place within a clear, agreed framework and that there is a clear end in view. Students are asked to read as many books as they can in the time available and to keep a short record. They are also asked to keep brief notes, which may take the form of a journal in which they write down their perceptions, their reflections. On the other hand they may choose to put more of their time into a piece of writing, which may be fiction or autobiographical, in which they explore what it is like to be living now, here, at this age. Everyone is asked to produce one piece of some length. Pupils are asked to choose incidents, characters, places, which say a lot in a little about life now. Again, the contrast with normal practice is quite deliberate. It is not too extreme a parody to say that the usual approach to writing means that no single piece lasts more than two weeks, most are 'done' within the week. Teachers often complain that their pupils do not have the stamina to develop a long piece, and if they do it is of poorer quality than their usual shorter pieces. Only writing at length will develop the capacity to write at length – no amount of preparation for it will secure sustained concentration, though clear purpose will help. Also the degree of organisation required can only be developed with a good deal of running support from a more skilled practitioner, the teacher. It is no good expecting a student to labour away for weeks and then submit a completed piece, untainted by critical interchange. Sometimes that will succeed; more often what is submitted has broken down for lack of sympathetic reading (that is where good marking begins and ends) at the right time. The writing I am suggesting will seek to explore a chosen area at some length in narrative form, probably using the pattern of a series of key events as images. There will have usually been a conscious choice of the images, which will be discussed with the teacher at an appropriate time. During the writing the teacher should keep in touch with developments, ready to intercede if necessary. (There will also be a need to be proof-reading editor as well, perhaps suggesting rewriting of parts that are obscure, just badly written, or in need of tidying up. Though the 'decencies' of spelling and punctuation are subservient to a larger purpose, they should not be forgotten.) There will be redrafting at times, so the writing is best done on loose-leaf paper so that sections can be taken out, put in, changed around, in the way that any real writing needs to be (as indeed has this chapter). Students can, if they prefer, work in a group to (a) read a book, (b) write a play, (c) explore in drama the experience they choose, or (d) record a reading.

The end of all these pursuits is to present to the class something which takes the discussion on into greater complexity and greater confidence. Sometimes the 'presentation' will be merely a piece of writing pinned on the wall; at other times the class will be invited to borrow a tape if they are interested. The aim should be to allow a variety of responses and a choice about how public that should be. Any class will contain students who prefer reticence and our way of working should not threaten it too much.

Some agility is required on the part of the teacher to point up connections where they occur, to draw together those who are working on similar themes and who might benefit from exchange. On the other hand, care needs to be taken not to steer the whole enterprise along an overdefined path. If work of this kind is to be at all real some of the directions taken will not be predictable. The most characteristic lesson will be one during which there is hardly any talk; most are reading silently, making occasional notes, or are absorbed in a piece of writing, while the teacher slowly moves along from person to person, drawing out, putting in. The teacher needs to be aware in detail of what pupils are working on if the advice offered is to be suitable. Too often we teachers assume a broad kind of advice is suitable enough for most of the class. The width of interest and approach in this kind of work means that precise acquaintance is a prerequisite of good individual advice. Of course, sometimes the best response is silence (though there are qualities of silence).

Exchange and Presentation

Before many weeks have elapsed, some of the directions being taken by the students will be clearly emerging. The reading will be, under guidance from the teacher, following a thread; the writing will probably have begun, yet still be tentative and sporadic until the whole scheme becomes clear in the mind. At this stage one session a week should be devoted to class exchange, during which students are asked to tell each other what they think so far. Here recommendations for further reading can be given. It is the time also for some improvised drama where there is some emerging topic of interest, during which situations that illustrate the topic are explored in groups. The aim is to give further insights which can be brought to reading, writing and discussion.

In the last weeks, the teacher needs to negotiate a timetable for the more formal presentations. The final stage of all is to draw the whole class together to discuss and decide upon, if possible, some five novels that they feel speak for the world they recognise. The teacher may be disappointed with the choice, but it is not the aim to have the students choosing what the teacher wanted. Once a choice is made, the teacher may comment on the books chosen, but beware the implication of putting the matter right. The tone of this comment will be surer where there has been a proper interchange during the work. It may be argued that this choice of five books is a very artificial matter, and so it is. The purpose is not to identify the choice, but to go through the process of making a choice over a period of time, and to marshal the evidence to make that appraisal.

Conclusion

This scheme of work as an approach to literature in the fourth year offers a number of things that I think are worth having:

It balances individual reading with group activity; they interact positively.

It gives time to read and write in depth.

Reading, writing and talk interact in a genuinely purposeful way.

The students can relate the product of a writer to their own writing.

Both the private and public worlds of the learner are given space and respect.

However there are problems. There is a great temptation for the teacher to lead too early, to shut down alternatives. Even in writing up the description I have given here, the giving of specific examples is in danger of fixing what should be a rather fluid way of working. The descriptions of classroom work that are easiest to follow clearly are those where the teacher is being didactic. Where there is a repeated shift between teacher intervention and pupil autonomy there will always be some degree of unpredictability. It is a living kind of teaching if there is a living kind of learning.

The scheme of literature work I have outlined is only part of a year's study. At other times there will be class readers, poetry and plays read together, a lot of individualised reading. I do not intend that there should only be one kind of reading. There should be a wide variety of approaches; this one merits a more regular place than it often has.

References

DONALDSON, M. (1978) *Children's Minds* (Fontana)
WALKER, C. (1974) *Reading Development and Extension* (Ward Lock)

8 Film and Television in the English Lesson

John M. P. Hodgson

'Film and television in the English lesson? They'd be better off learning to read and write. They get more than enough television at home, anyway.'

This kind of rejoinder over staff-room coffee is understandable and to be expected, and any teacher who proposes to show his students a film or television programme should be clear about his reasons. As English teachers, our primary concern is with language, as a means of intellectual and emotional growth. How, then, can we justify the use of largely visual media in our classrooms?

'Language,' John Dixon (1967) has said, 'is learned in operation . . . in English, pupils meet to share their encounters with life.' Certain films and television programmes can bring 'life' into the classroom with a directness which compels students to feel, imagine, think, and to find the language to express their responses. The following piece of writing was produced by a fourth year student after her 'encounter' with a Thames Television English programme, *The Price of Tin*, about the lives of tin-miners in Bolivia:

> Another day dawns. Pedro is awakened by the sound of a church bell . . .
> In the half-light he sees his six children asleep, huddled together for warmth in a cold corner. His wife is ill under the strain of having six children between the ages of two and thirteen, and having hardly any food.
> Pedro feels bad about leaving her, but it would be worse if he did not go to work. His weekly income is £7, but most of this is taken in social security and repayment of debts . . .
>
> *Emily*

I cite this not as an outstanding piece of work, but as an example of a response which shows the writer's unaffected engagement with the film. She has been moved by the miners' lives, and has also understood the immediate cause of their suffering: she remembers details of their income. The mention of the church bell seems to suggest, too, awareness of the influence of religion on the lives of the miners and their families.

Viewing *The Price of Tin* was part of a half-term unit of work with an 'able' fourth year group, in which my aim was to demonstrate that the poetic is not a specialised form of language but an element in many different kinds of effective communication. We started by viewing the first programme in the Thames series *I See a Voice*, which illustrates several functions of poetic statement. I then involved the class in a variety of reading, writing and reciting which deliberately emphasised the pleasure that can be gained from working with language. The description of Stradhoughton in *Billy Liar* (1959) led us to produce tourists' guides (sometimes ironical) to Devon:

> This majestic looking town, situated on one of the highest parts of Dartmoor, is built around the famous Dartmoor prison, with its original granite walls proudly dominating the area . . .
>
> *Ian*

Billy Fisher's song-writing inspired us to write parodies of popular numbers (we sang some of the best ones):

> It's a long way to the goal-mouth;
> It's a long way to shoot.
> It's a long way to the goal-mouth
> And there's a goalie there, to boot!
>
> *Claudia*

Some Clare poems depicting winter ('The Foddering Boy' was especially liked) prompted writing about the current season. At this stage, I wanted to suggest the power of language to render experience in order to stir others to 'mental fight'. We read Wilfred Owen, lingering especially on 'The Send-off' and 'The Sentry', after which I introduced some poems by Pablo Neruda, the Chilean writer. *The Price of Tin* (and the following films in the 'One World' series) gave a context for Neruda's words:

> His struggle was with water or with earth . . .
> perhaps the one who did not come home
> because water or earth drowned him
> or a machine or tree killed him . . .

The class were clearly moved by the film, and I wanted to help them find a way of writing which both focused their thoughts and permitted each individual to express his or her response. The simple title *The Price of Tin* seems to have served this purpose. The phrase seems to have acted as what Witkin (1974) calls a 'holding form', clarifying for the writer his primary emotional impulse, and allowing him to go on to express this impulse in his unique way.

Emily's engagement made her want to choose narrative. Ian was especially struck by the larger causes of the people's suffering, and tried to clarify them for himself and his reader in writing:

> All the suffering I have mentioned comes from the fact that Bolivia is a very unstable country politically (on average one coup occurs every year) and tin which is the basis of the Bolivian economy has a very unstable price, due to the consumer countries such as Britain and America

deciding the price . . . Bolivia is also in debt to these countries so the country has to supply them with tin at whatever price or quantity the countries she is in debt to, want . . .

Ian

The Price of Tin is formally a very direct and simple programme. The camera observes the miners at work or at home (nothing seems to have been reconstructed for the camera); the men and women tell Jonathan Dimbleby about their lives, and he provides a factual commentary. It is this commentary, supported by the images, which provides most of the emotion and experience that motivate and inform the writing of the class:

> The black dust down the mines causes silicosis, a disease which attacks the lungs and shortens life expectancy considerably . . . When the miner dies the Company will heartlessly turn his wife and children from their home to make way for an able-bodied worker . . .
>
> *Helen*

This kind of writing seems to me to demonstrate the contribution that film and television can make to English work. A well-chosen film is not simply a visual experience: like good literature, it can create new awareness, and affect the student's (and teacher's) way of thinking and feeling. *The Price of Tin* gives experience of life far removed from our students' own, in a way that provokes response. It provides both matter and motive for expression.

My criteria in choosing a film (to use the convenient term – I include television programmes) for use in class are essentially the same as those I apply in choosing written material. Does this film offer me genuine insight, make me think, suggest new ways of seeing, make me feel differently? In other words, is it art? If I can regard it as such, my own interest in the material will be conveyed to the class. Art, in this definition, has nothing to do with preconceived notions of culture, nor with the dishonesty (however 'well expressed') of advertising and propaganda; nor does it exclude non-fictional material. *The Price of Tin* is art in the same sense that George Orwell's *Down the Mine* is art, and I use it in class for the same reasons.

Or for nearly the same reasons. For, of course, film has the advantage over print of providing more accessible experience for many students. This most certainly does not mean that it should be used within 'English' as a substitute for reading. On the contrary, it can be used to encourage and extend reading: a fourth year girl I teach told me recently that she was reading *Brideshead Revisited* while watching the television serial, then being presented (1981). Her method was to watch one episode and then, with a friend, to read and discuss the corresponding chapters of the novel. She never read ahead of the television version, because the programme helped her to imagine what she read.

We should not undervalue the service that film and television can do here. My fifth form CSE group have read with pleasure and comprehension substantial episodes from *Far from the Madding Crowd* alongside the film. Other films which I have found useful in the same way include *A Kind of Loving* and *To Kill a Mockingbird*, while schools television productions of *Macbeth*, *Juno and the Paycock* and *The Long and the Short and the Tall* have all helped my students imagine their respective texts.

Film within a Term's English Work

I have suggested above that a film can be more than a visual aid to reading: it can be a 'text' in its own right within a term's English programme, each of the works studied throwing light on and extending the significance of the others. Musing recently upon *Lord of the Flies* (1955), which is a frequently prescribed text, I felt that I could not merely teach the book without introducing any complementary material. I have found that some of the significance of the novel is not readily apparent to students, and I believe that they should have the opportunity to evaluate the view of human nature implied by Golding.

To remind the class of some of the facts behind Golding's pessimism, I decided to read with them Peter Weiss's essay 'My Place'. Weiss describes the reactions of a Jew who evaded Auschwitz and visited the camp for the first time twenty tears after the war. This honest piece of writing moves by its lack of passion: Weiss recounts that the mute solidity of the ruins did not create for him the visions of his previous reading about the camp.

Another aspect of the book on which I wanted to enlarge is the character of Simon, who often seems overshadowed in readers' minds by the other characters and events. Simon's mode of being seems similar to that which Wordsworth celebrates in the early books of *The Prelude*; and one Wordsworth poem – the fragment 'Nutting' – contains imagery very similar to that of *Lord of the Flies*:

> Then up I rose,
> And dragged to earth both branch and bough, with crash
> And merciless ravage . . .

This links well with the moment (towards the end of Chapter One of *Lord of the Flies*) when Jack, Simon and Ralph's differing responses to the 'candle buds' defines their attitudes to 'the world'. Golding's concern here could be further illuminated, I felt, by some works by Lawrence, such as his poem 'Snake' and essay 'Reflections on the Death of a Porcupine'.

It was while thinking of Wordsworth that I remembered the following passage from *The Wild Boy of Aveyron* (1977), Harlan Lane's account of Jean Itard's education of the feral boy discovered in France in 1797:

All those spasmodic movements and continual swaying of his whole body diminished, subsiding by degrees and giving way to a more tranquil attitude; . . . his face, vacant or grimacing, imperceptibly took on a decidedly sad or melancholy expression, as his eyes clung fixedly to the surface of the water, while from time to time he threw in some debris or dry leaves.

This reminded me of Truffaut's film about the boy, *L'Enfant Sauvage*, which I had previously shown in school. This, I felt, would provide an ideal complement to *Lord of the Flies*.

The novel presents a conception of human society as repressing and disguising the Beast in Man. Truffaut offers a different approach to the relation between nature and nurture. We are shown the socialisation and education of Victor, the 'natural' boy, as Itard (played by Truffaut in the film) works remorselessly to teach him language and behaviour. The film's viewpoint seems somewhat similar to that of Truffaut's earlier *Les 400 Coups* (which I have also shown most successfully in school) in its presentation of the destructive power of social experience (some of Blake's poems, such as 'The Schoolboy', are relevant here, and go well with students of varying abilities). Yet Truffaut does not give a simple image of a child of nature chained by society. Before his capture, the boy seems less than human, shivering and alone; he can become human only by entering the 'human world' of consciousness. (One of the failings of Truffaut's Itard is that he regards language as learned primarily through external teaching, rather than through the growing human's need to make sense of his world.)

L'Enfant Sauvage grips my students, perhaps because they identify with Victor in his schoolroom! Through this film, it is possible to open up the central question of *Lord of the Flies* – answered with perhaps too much confidence by Golding – in terms that are not too abstract for the fifteen-year-old. The same question can be explored further by means of extracts from Margaret Mead's *Sex and Temperament in Three Primitive Societies* (1935), which demonstrate the effects of culture in creating 'natural' behaviour. Margaret Mead describes the upbringing from infancy of the gentle Arapesh and hostile Mundugumor tribes of New Guinea. I always find that these passages raise enormous interest in class: both boys and girls are fascinated by accounts of the early life-experience by which we 'build up the being that we are' (the childhood episodes from *The Prelude* appeal for the same reason).

The reader will have little difficulty in thinking of further material which might be linked with *Lord of the Flies*. I recall a recent BBC 'Play for Today', *Shadows on our Skin*, based on the novel by Jennifer Johnston, which evokes the mutual fear and hostility of the factions in Northern Ireland as experienced by a young Roman Catholic boy. Unlike *Lord of the Flies*, the play locates the violence within a social context.

It will be seen that the course of work outlined here is not a loose thematic linking of disparate material. The films, poems and prose passages are intended both to illuminate and develop the significance of *Lord of the Flies* and to offer a more inclusive approach to the issues with which the book is concerned. Each extract, poem or film will be considered fully in its own right, and not subordinated to any overall 'theme'. Study may take the form of whole-class discussion closely focused upon a particular moment of the text (here print has the advantage over film that it can, so to speak, be instantly replayed, although videotape can fairly easily be rewound); or the class may work individually or in small discussion-groups, with questions to guide their attention to various points in the text. I sometimes ask individuals and groups to frame their own questions: this can increase genuine reflection on the text, with less concern for a quick answer.

The purpose of this close attention is so that, in Witkin's (1974) words, 'the individual [can] find his way in [the text], explore all its possibilities, or, more correctly, all the possibilities it has for him.' Witkin's self-correction here seems important. We must insist on the student's attention to and reflection on the text, but we cannot impose a 'correct' reading, for a response which is not personal is valueless.

A genuine – that is, personal – response to a book, film or other art-experience may naturally prompt expression in a creative mode, rather than a critical-analytical formulation. (This is instanced by my students' responses to *The Price of Tin* – and not only by Emily's narrative piece.) I find it important, therefore, to try to set assignments which help students to channel their thoughts in their individual way. Sometimes one well-chosen title will do this, as *The Price of Tin* did for my students; sometimes it helps to suggest alternatives. Always it is necessary to walk around the class and discuss with individuals their own methods of approach.

Here, then, are examples of writing topics based on *L'Enfant Sauvage*. As a group they are intended to be appropriate to the range of emotional and intellectual development shown by the class: students can choose whichever suits their way of thinking.

1   Imagine you are one of the young people in the village where the wild boy is taken after his capture. You watch him being brought into the village by the men with dogs. Later you creep into the barn where he is chained up . . .

2   You are a man or woman living in a remote village. You hear that a wild boy has been found and decide to adopt him. Describe the first day he lives with you.

3   If you took on the task of looking after a 'wild child', what would you do? How would your methods differ from Itard's?

4   Write a story about a boy or girl who is abandoned by his or her parents, telling what happens to him/her in the wild. (It may help to write as if you are the child.)

5   What do you think the life of the boy in the wild would have been like? Describe how he would have lived, and compare this with life in society. Which would you prefer?

Study of the Medium

At best, students' art-response to a film or television 'text' – such as *The Price of Tin* essays – will show change in their ways of thinking and feeling. It is not only 'quality' programmes, however, which influence viewers; mass communications generally, of which television is one form, are a source of a good part of the experience and ideas of our students and ourselves. For this reason, I believe that a study of the language which our students daily absorb from the principal mass media – television and the press – should form part of 'English' work in the latter years of secondary education. To illustrate a possible means of studying the 'language' of television, I shall give a brief account of aspects of a three-week course with a fourth year class centred on television news.

Every aspect of our environment carries socially given meaning: we learn the significance of others' gestures, of their clothes, of the rooms they inhabit. In communicating its messages, television, as a visual medium, makes use of these meanings. Before a class begins to look at an everyday television programme, then, there is some essential preliminary work to be done: the study of visual imagery, in order to make conscious some of the learned meanings that make up our common sense view of the world.

The significance of people's *posture* and *gestures* can be enjoyably discussed by means of a charade-like game in which members of the class mime such emotions as apathy, anger, confidence, anxiety, self-blame, aggressiveness, tiredness, friendliness, and so on. In interpreting the bodily states portrayed, it is important that the class describe the clues as precisely as possible. Tiredness, for example, may be signified not only by the obvious slumped posture, but also by such details as forehead-wiping.

Relationships between people can be deduced in part from their *closeness* and *orientation* to each other. Again, it is easy to devise a game to examine these features. Two students enact, without words, an interview, a candle-lit dinner, a chat between two close friends, a conversation where one is bored by the other, teacher and class, a young person being cautioned in a police station. The class attempt to deduce the situation, considering the participants' closeness to each other, whether they are facing, side by side, or at an angle to each other, and the importance of any physical barrier. Here, too, posture and gesture form part of the meaning of the situation: the participants in both the interview and the dinner will tend to face each other, but the situations will be distinguishable not only by a difference in closeness but also by alterations in the way the participants hold their bodies and move their heads and limbs.

To discuss the meaning of *physical appearance* and *facial expression*, I like to bring into the class someone the students are unlikely to have met, who sits silently while observed for clues to indicate such matters as age, sex, occupation, and personality.

All this work can be consolidated by a piece of observational writing centred on a photograph. The preceding activities should help to sharpen students' perception, and the language with which they record this, and make a not uncommon exercise more than usually fruitful.

Objects too provide a focus for students' written or spoken analysis. The lesson is easily prepared: on a recent occasion, it took me five minutes to pick up from my home a collection which included a child's sewing-machine, a Silver Jubilee tea-tin, and a wine bottle. To prompt responses, I ask pupils to describe the object carefully; to say why they think it is as it is (the reasons may be functional or ideological: the tea-tin efficiently excludes air and odours, yet the very method of keeping tea in a tin is redolent of an essential aspect of 'Englishness', of which Royalty, pictured on the container, is the supreme symbol); and to express all the associations (connotations) it has for them. This exercise, like the previous ones, sits easily within the English lesson; students observe and describe to increase their consciousness of the meanings we give our world.

Exercises such as these prepare for discussion of the visual aspect of television. In studying the *News*, I start with the title sequence:

> The ITN *News at Ten* title reflects the fact that the news is gathered from all over the world by showing landmarks of four major cities . . .
>
> *Sue*

The lesson on the meaning of objects perhaps bears fruit in comments on Big Ben:

> Big Ben is shown striking ten o'clock to symbolise parliament and government news. It also reassures the public that Parliament is still standing . . .
>
> *Jon*

And the discussion of personal appearance and of physical closeness seems reflected in this student's comments on the news-reader:

> The news-reader has grey hair and wears a suit. He gives the impression of being in authority. This is also because he looks like he is across a desk from us.
>
> *Mark*

At least as important as the visual language of the *News* is the verbal. Transcribing broadcast speech is difficult, and so for this aspect of the work I usually turn to the Press. Peter Abbs' *English Broadsheet* (1971) 'Newspapers Today' offers a simple introduction to the study of the affective power of language; he gives three descriptions of the same incident, and asks students to define the attitude each implies towards the participants. From here I turn to duplicated extracts from newspapers, and discuss with students the way the language works. A letter to the *Guardian* by Philip Kingston (1981) gives an idea of the kind of analysis involved:

> Polaris sounds like a baby polar bear; Trident is a symbol of Britannia or Neptune and a weapon that would appear to do little damage – rather like

a not very effective gardening fork . . . Cruise missiles appear to be a combination of holidays and a means of travelling to the moon . . . These [associations] are underwritten by a further sleight-of-hand: that it will all take place in a 'theatre' of war . . .

All the work described above is concerned with helping students to grasp the way in which the medium affects the messages received by the viewer. In studying the *News*, however, one must also draw attention to the fact that millions of possible messages are not transmitted; one must consider the criteria by which a few items are daily selected as 'news'. This can be enjoyably done by means of a simulation.

A useful simulation of a radio news broadcast, 'Radio Covingham', is available commercially; or the teacher can prepare the materials, using the local paper as the source of news. Splitting the class into groups of between seven and ten individuals, one tells each group that they are a radio or television team who have to prepare a ten minute 'News and Views' programme to go out in, say, seventy-five minutes. (A substantial block of time is preferable for this work; spreading it over two or three days reduces the urgency which is essential to the news-room atmosphere.) At the start of their preparation period, each team is given a collection of letters, press releases and news items which have come in 'overnight'; they can start selecting items for the programme, editing and rewriting them, but they will have to be constantly readjusting their schedule of items as the day's news from agencies and reporters flows into the room. These further items are provided by the teacher (in role as office messenger) at intervals, until each group has perhaps a dozen possible 'stories' (in addition to letters, press releases, and so on). The last one, received twenty minutes before the programme goes on the air, can be of sufficient 'importance' for the team to have to find a way of including it. It is important to emphasise to each group that their *News*, like the professional version, should include interviews and expert comment as well as the newcasters' presentation. One should also insist that the programme must be *exactly* ten minutes in length, and to this end a memorandum from the Station Manager can be distributed, complaining about sloppy timing the previous day.

What can be learned from such a simulation? To produce a successful 'broadcast', pupils have to précis reports to an appropriate length (and, in so doing, they realise the relative brevity of the spoken, compared with the written, report); they have to speak to an anonymous 'public'; they have to interview or be interviewed. Further, the simulation promotes a felt understanding of aspects of the process of news selection and presentation. If the preparatory session can itself be unobtrusively tape recorded, or overheard by the teacher, it will reveal the making of numerous significant decisions. A recent session in my own classroom included the following: that the news-reader should be a boy; that the generally depressing range of items chosen for inclusion should be 'balanced' by a 'happy' final story; that an interviewee (manager of a local company planning to expand its premises) should be told in advance what questions to expect. Discussion of the unconscious reasons behind such decisions can bring home to the participants that, contrary to appearances, interesting news does not arise naturally out of the world.

One might conclude a study of television news by showing and discussing a programme in Thames Television's 'Viewpoint 2' series, *Real to Reel*. This deals amusingly with such matters as the obscure language in which business and industrial news is presented; the narrative construction of news in terms of villains and victims; and, most importantly, the function of the *News* in 'defining for people what the important issues are and the terms in which they should be discussed' (Hartmann and Husband, 1971).

Conclusion

Readers who wish to pursue the kind of work on the 'language' of television described in the preceding section will find assistance from some of the books listed below and from the Education Department of the British Film Institute. The necessary brevity of my account should underline my conviction that analysis of an everyday television programme is a complement to, not a substitute for, response to those programmes (and films) which can be termed art. These affect the student's being; and in his own art-response, he reacts from his whole self, and not only with the analytical faculty which is involved in a study of the medium. If the latter study makes for awareness and criticism of the images of the 'world' conveyed by mass communications, art-response can be a means of discovering 'a new world within the known world'.

Bibliography

This includes every book mentioned in the text, and a few others which I have found especially useful.

ABBS, P. (1971) *English Broadsheets, Series II* (Heinemann)
ARGYLE, M. (1967) *The Psychology of Interpersonal Behaviour* (Penguin)
BARTHES, R. (1972) *Mythologies* (Cape)
COHEN, S. and YOUNG. J. (1973) *The Manufacture of News* (Constable)
DIXON, J. (1967) *Growth through English* (Oxford University Press)
GOLDING, P. (1974) *The Mass Media* (Longman)
GOLDING, W. (1955) *Lord of the Flies* (Faber)
HARTMANN, P. and HUSBAND, C. (1971) 'The Mass Media and Racial Conflict' in COHEN, S. and YOUNG, J. op. cit.
HAYAKAWA, S. I. (1952) *Language in Thought and Action* (Allen and Unwin)
HOOD, S. (1980) *On Television* (Pluto Press)
HUNT, A. (1981) *The Language of Television* (Eyre Methuen)

KINGSTON, P. (1981) letter in *The Guardian*, February 7; reprinted in Tunnicliffe, S. 'English and Nuclear War' in *The Use of English*, Volume 32, No. 3, pages 3–9

LANE, H. (1979) *The Wild Boy of Aveyron* (Granada)

LAWRENCE, D. H. *Selected Essays* (Penguin, 1950)

LAWRENCE, D. H. *The Complete Poems of D. H. Lawrence* (ed.) MOORE, H. T. (Heinemann, 1964)

MEAD, M. (1935) *Sex and Temperament in Three Primitive Societies* (Routledge and Kegan Paul)

MORRIS, D. (1978) *Manwatching* (Granada)

NERUDA, P. (1975) *Selected Poems* (ed.) TARN, N. (Penguin)

WATERHOUSE, K. (1959) *Billy Liar* (Michael Joseph)

WEISS, P., 'My Place' in *German Writing Today* (Penguin, 1967)

WITKIN, R. W. (1974) *The Intelligence of Feeling* (Heinemann)

WORDSWORTH, W. *The Poetical Works of Wordsworth* (ed.) HUTCHINSON, T. (Oxford University Press, 1904)

The simulation 'Radio Covingham' is available from the ILEA Media Resources Centre, Highbury Station Road, Islington, London N1 1SB.

All films available for hire within Great Britain are listed in the catalogue *Films on Offer*, published annually by the British Film Institute, 81 Dean Street, London W1V 6AA.

The Society for Education in Film and Television, 29 Old Compton Street, London W1V 5PL, provides a journal for teachers interested in film and television study, and organises courses and conferences, sometimes in collaboration with the Education Department of the British Film Institute (address as above).

9 Towards Public Issues: An English Programme for 14 to 16 Years

Malcolm Stanton

Great literature is indeed enriching, liberating and refining, but man is always and everywhere more than a reader, has indeed to be a great deal else before he can even become an adequate reader . . .

Raymond Williams, Culture and Society (1958)

. . . the inextricable interrelations between politics, art, economics, family organisation . . .
Raymond Williams, Politics and Letters (1980)

Realising that every teaching act reflects a tacit theory I shall clarify briefly my assumptions about English studies as a process and a product. This is one way of explaining the organising principles behind the classroom work I describe.

In exploring the human meanings of a subject such as 'War', for instance, I am building upon a department tradition where the daily practice has been to find a correspondence between the language/ consciousness of the pupil and the art/ideology of the cultural materials we can discover and employ. This begins in Year One by accepting and fostering the pupil's own language resources; it extends, by Year Three, to confront deliberately the 'public domain' and therefore public languages, official and unofficial, artistic and functional. Since the majority of our pupils are rural working class we have to search for the best means of 'informing' (offering 'art-works' that are demanding but relevant) and 'discovering' (finding and giving their voices a place and status in the learning). What, then, is the rationale for choosing as we do; and what kinds of control and autonomy can operate for the student and teacher? Above all, what aims does this approach fulfil?

English Studies as Cultural Engagement

Through our native language(s) we may express most vitally, and communicate most effectively our sense of place in the world. Language as a manifestation of our being, doing and becoming, is indeed a social and material 'activity'. But the important emphasis in language development, made crucial by Vygotsky (in *Thought and Language*, 1962) is the socio-historical, the stress upon the simultaneous individual and social presence of humans in the world. It follows that its teaching in schools, its actual verbal practice, be manifestly cultural. Trained mostly in a specialised aesthetic dimension, the national literature, the teacher of English is bound to rely upon that 'knowledge' as the most central ground for teaching and learning. Within that practice reside all the familiar arguments about 'value' and relative 'autonomy'.

As my account of work will show, I am not disengaging from literature or art-works; but I am trying to reforge the links between 'texts' and the everyday uses of our language in its personal and its public modes. The heart of a lesson may be the meanings that pupils can make of Keith Douglas' seminal 'Vergissmeinnicht'; it may be the meanings they can bring, through imagination and wondering, to the real rifle bayonet and German war helmet I display before them. There is nothing unusual about this sort of classroom engagement. The best primary schools, for instance, have always sought to introduce 'phenomena' from the outside world to be shown, touched, tasted, smelt, or heard; but always the act of learning and understanding begins with attention. We realise that literary/artistic activity-production is significant only through a process of gradual immersion in it, alongside many sorts of other cultural experiencing. Nor can the committed teacher use the classroom as either music-hall for florid entertainment or as a lecture theatre for the latest treatise upon, say, a hedonistic society. The further, intrinsic danger is not to let the 'theme' (a selected form of organisation that prefaces 'values') become the McLuhan-like 'message' to imprison the pupil's mind. On the other side of this dilemma the teacher has to have some laudable aims in the broad categories of aesthetic, social and political education.

The institutional nature of our task makes us mediators, creating dialogues between teacher, 'culture', culture-in-the-making and pupil. This mediating involves adopting art-works as 'practices' as well as manifest 'objects'; it shifts the emphasis to meanings which are created by the artist, responded to and remade into meanings by the pupils. There still remains in our pattern some space for autonomy, for small scale attempts to create, in Harold Rosen's phrase, 'collaborative productions of meanings . . .' ('Neither Bleak House nor Liberty Hall', 1981). It is in the 'English' classroom that perhaps this can happen quite overtly, given the multidimensional quality and character of the thinking and communication taking place. Such a dialogue is the core of English studies; it is the heart and life of thriving engagement.

The question about the role of literature in school might now be better dealt with as a matter of 'positioning' amongst other materials of comparable claim. I valued it on its own terms, not because it amplified a study. It was at specific moments in the classroom an intense experience, an extension of minds and imaginations quite irreplaceable and irreducible, never an evasion of other possible or immediate connections. A host of factors governed its priority in the eventual sequence of lessons, from the encountered mood of students to the need to communicate, as only art can so 'artfully' do, a particular and peculiar feel of things.

What I envisaged to be at the centre of the study, what I hoped would count most, was the perception that the real nature of war could best be understood by unifying our own responses to its available evidence and descriptions. Literature and art became part of that continuity of our making sense of experiences beyond us. It had, in the midst of all our encounters, to accommodate us; and we had to accommodate it, as we reached for new meanings and relationships at its pulse.

The ensuing organisational frame, short and long term, grew out of the need to synthesise, and, overall, to seek a balance between knowledge offered and knowledge to be made.

A Common CSE Course: Its Organisation and Context

The department devised the syllabus with several local schools. We continue to meet as a consortium to discuss our teaching, and to assess students under the guidance of an external moderator. Although the continuous assessment course is split (regrettably) into 'Language' and 'Literature' components in order to qualify for dual certification, our teaching patterns retain a unity here. At the end of the course the students' files are divided into separate areas of study, the 'Language' comprising 70 per cent writing (fifteen varied pieces) and 30 per cent oral, the 'Literature' being 100 per cent writing (fifteen varied pieces according to literary criteria). As in the first three years the groups remain mixed ability but are rotated each term amongst the teachers so that a diverse range of work is taught freshly. By the fifth term in Year Five there is some regrouping for about the final fifteen weeks, as students wishing to take 'O' Level Language enter a 'crash course'. ('O' Level Literature is taken as an option in Years Four and Five.) Consequently teachers plan termly or half-termly schemes which are usually thematic in contents and structure. We talk through our material needs and advance plans, so that we have in mind a certain body and direction of work. Naturally, we take into account that adjustments will be necessary, but we are aware of our personal styles, resources and methods. Rotating the groups also means we can share thoughts about students' attitudes, interests, abilities, and about teaching successes and failures.

In a department which is committed to English studies as a learning medium about 'cultural processes' it is important to retain continuity in 'content' and procedure from Year One to Year Seven. We retain a strong sense of the spiralling nature of methods and materials for teachers and students. Work in Years Four and Five is different mainly in intellectual terms from that in Years One, Two and Three. Then in Years Six and Seven there is either the 'A' Level Literature Alternative

Syllabus piloted by the Associated Examining Board (AEB) in regional consortia, including some course work and open book exams as well as a broadening content, or a new 'O/A' Level course for one or two years in 'English'.

The distinctive feature of the common CSE course is its outwardness: a directing of thought and practice upon major public matters. In that case our 'themes' have to be compelling. They have to be inclusive and open, as well as balanced in variety of tasks and skills required. What follows is a description of a 'topic' of study I undertook with a class of twenty-six students in the first term of the fifth year. It took approximately twelve weeks (lessons are 70 minutes and there are five on a fortnightly timetable), but the sequence included refreshment breaks for private reading.

The Experience of War: A CSE English Study

The structure which, ostensibly, I kept in my mind and planned from was historical and chronological. My aim was that the students should gradually fill in a shape which would become clearer as the cultural materials cohered in their minds. They could remould it but we still had to make sense of it together in the end. Certain items were centrally important, and, initially, for the whole group, while others were simply available, negotiable, or dispensable. I wanted the whole class to read as much of Stephen Crane's *The Red Badge of Courage* as they could enjoy, and the whole of Remarque's *All Quiet on the Western Front*; the whole year-group were also due to see the film version of the latter. There would be further readings of poems and short stories, journalism and biography; viewings of paintings and photographs; listening to recordings – all as a class-group. This had to be so for reasons of teaching and of planning. The nature of the subject and its urgency, the time available and the necessary marking and monitoring for assess-ment purposes, the necessity to understand extreme experience far removed from their lives (and, of course, never to be repeated), all led to regular joint reception and response. It was therefore essential to build in duly available materials and tasks and spaces for individuals and groups. Ultimately, through sharing and moving in and out of a range of art and artefacts, I was aiming for a consciousness of war as the most extreme event in terms of scale and impact known to mankind. Some notion of the inevitability of war, of its changing technology, its patterns and shocks, and most crucially, its results in human terms, could only be sensed via a continuous input of varied but intensively felt material.

We began with a pile of comics spread around the tables. The most lurid, such as *Battle Picture Weekly*, were disavowed but in fact closely read by the boys. Girls complained about their subjection to 'a boy's subject' but soon talk generated questions about realism of image and narrative, and finally about what a truer representation of warfare would amount to. There was time to move on to the first chapter of *The Red Badge of Courage* as I suggested we read some war stories and they talk to close relations about their possible war experiences. This would mean, for them, finding grandparents or the more elderly.

At the start of our second lesson I introduced a large format book of war pictures, Thomas' *Battle Art: Images of War* (1977) and retained the visual emphasis by getting small groups to compare this historical vision with the specific Second World War 'cartoon' imagery in the comics, again available. The visually symbolic demands of Goya in his stunning *Disasters of War* series moved us on to more reading of *The Red Badge of Courage* and notably the youth's first encounter of battle. The students had to read more on their own in preparation for next week's lesson, as well as return with war anecdotes from relations. I should explain here that students were also expected to be reading from books available in the school library, or from my class library box in the classroom, or from home. There would be set times for private reading in the classroom. The war theme was not to be relentlessly pursued as I tried to explain in the earlier description of the context of CSE work.

With three lessons in the second week there would be time to focus on the text, so I got the whole class to look closely at some key passages in Stephen Crane's novel. Never an easy book, written in a superficially objective way, highly metaphorical but also verbally demanding for a fifteen or sixteen-year-old, and 'archaic' in its contents dealing with the primitive clashes of arms and the psychological responses to violent events, it nevertheless can evoke powerfully the moment of fear or revulsion or puzzlement, as an ordinary mind grapples with the extraordinary and seemingly uncontrollable events of arms. Crane's imagery using all the senses has its direct appeal to the younger reader, as the following extracts show:

The flames bit him and the hot smoke broiled his skin. His rifle barrel grew so hot that ordinarily he could not have borne it upon his palms; but he kept on stuffing cartridges into it, and pounding them with his clanking, bending ramrod. If he aimed at some changing form through the smoke, he pulled his trigger with a fierce grunt, as if he were dealing a blow of the fist with all his strength . . . (page 116)

His eyes still kept note of the clump of trees. From all places near it the clannish yell of the enemy could be heard. The little flames of rifles leapt from it. The song of the bullets was in the air and shells snarled among the treetops. One tumbled directly into the middle of a hurrying group and exploded in a crimson fury. There was an instant's spectacle of a man, almost over it, throwing up his hands to shield his eyes.

Other men, punched by bullets, fell in grotesque agonies. The regiment left a coherent trail of bodies . . . (page 126)

Tottering among them was the rival colour bearer, whom the youth saw had been bitten vitally by the bullets of the last formidable volley. He perceived this man fighting a last struggle, the struggle of one whose legs are grasped by demons. It was a ghastly battle. Over his face was the bleach of death, but set upon it was the dark and hard lines of desperate purpose . . . (page 152)

The Red Badge of Courage, 1964 edition.

The students were able to compare this to the crude and minimal linguistic and imaginative demands of 'balloon' dialogue in *Battle Picture Weekly*:

> 'Right – you've had enough training to know to be ready with that spare mag. I'm going to try an' hit the pilots.'
> 'Yes, Sir!'
> 'Here comes one now – and I'm aimin' slow and easy. Not scared are you Budd?'
> 'A bootneck Sir? Never.'
> 'Aaaaghhh! The rat's got me Budd! You're the number one – take over!'
> 'Right Sir! . . . You're gonna get the whole magazine Jerry!'
>
> (*page 13, 12 April 1975 issue*)

This was best done in pairs where they could attend to the words without too much help from me and then report in plenary about the differences between novel and comic. For this to have any critical pay-off there had to be sustained reading in each of that week's three lessons. I would narrate for a while or there would be a dramatised reading by some students. That way we got through two-thirds of the novel and the rest was voluntary. About fifteen of twenty-six students finished the text on their own. We agreed upon a range of writing tasks including creative and re-creative ones as a follow-up.

There was enough time at the start or towards the end of our seventy minute sessions to listen to reports of wartime experiences they had collected from relations. One boy brought in his father's flying gear – an oxygen mask, a scarf, gloves and helmet. To see this nearly forty years after the event, bruised from use by the rear gunner of a Lancaster, testament to a hundred nights of terror in the night clouds and on the German streets, gave resonance to our thinking about wars and their paraphernalia. It was made more poignant by the fact that the boy's father had written a moving, brief memoir of his fears as a gunner. He couldn't face coming into the classroom to talk to us; the memories were bitter. This led to a few more students involving relatives in their work; grans and grandads sent in anecdotes about German bombing raids or being wounded at the front. It didn't matter now that the chronology was broken – it was there in my mind still. The important leap had happened; they were closer to the realities of wars, and the gaps between the highly literary but virtual world of the text and the rough, resilient but realisable memoirs of the survivors, were closing. After all, out there on the streets of Wirksworth was 'Roy', the estranged survivor of a Second World War submarine disaster; a mumbling, shambling figure, ridiculed for his grumbling, repetitive speech. He was now their shuffling evidence that war doesn't have to kill to destroy. Crane had faced them with another reality too. Later we could compare the memories of the older teacher who came in to tell us about the desert war and they could read how Cecil Packwood (a marvellous man I'd met on holiday in Cornwall, born in 1900, who was on the Western Front at sixteen years of age) was shipped to France to join the infantry. Like many ordinary people he had begun to set down those pressing moments in a biographical way:

> We arrived at Rouen during the late afternoon and were quartered in army tents which were cheerless and cold in January. This camp was known as 'The Bull Ring' by the troops as it was here that army reinforcements were given their final severe training before proceeding to the front line. We were spared this ordeal as we were urgently needed reserves. The next morning we were conveyed in cattle trucks to a small village near the front line where we spent the night in an old barn. We could now hear the sound of gunfire and the next morning as we moved forward in lorries over the much-worn road the sound of gun-fire grew louder and louder. We now learned that we were being taken to the reserve line on the canal bank near Ypres. Suddenly we heard the scream of a shell which burst a short distance away and the time had come to go forward on foot through this dangerous area. This was it we thought as we walked in single file wondering where the next shell would land. As we gazed around us we could see the ravages of war on all sides. Dead artillery mules lay along the roadside, recently caught by shell fire. Tired troops walked wearily down the road on their way to rest camp. They were caked in mud and their gray faces plainly showed the strain of a stint at the front.

The link for these diverse voices was to be the literature of a more complex nature but it was not offered to be revered; more to be a link as we proceeded. So by the third week it was time to sharpen the focus. We split into three groups to read the American Civil War stories, *A Mystery of Heroism* and *The Upturned Face* by Stephen Crane, *An Occurrence at Owl Creek Bridge* by Ambrose Bierce. After reading independently each group had to come up with five questions about their particular story (while I remained a casual listener) placing initial emphasis upon content then moving out to meanings. These were then answered in detail in writing as part of a more literary package, including responses to the novel, for their files. The final lesson of the week centred on the film, *Incident at Owl Creek*. Those who had studied the original story were able to inform the rest about the differences, in terms of its artistic merits, between the two forms. Inevitably, and quite heatedly, this led to talk about the war films they were familiar with. Some students then preferred to write about these and their personal judgements rather than the recent stories. That was fine. I wanted self-chosen tasks to emerge. Any meandering students or the more reluctant did better here, and at least it gave them some hold on a subject that so far had been chosen for them. I had also made it clear that there were minimum expectations: some central material had to be considered but outside that I was relaxing the frame. Soon there would be much more flexibility in the study. Fortunately only a handful remained on the fringe but they were tolerant and admitted enjoying some items.

At the start of the fourth week we appraised work-in-progress, and I asked the students about how they would like to proceed. I also introduced a general guidance sheet and said I would add any tasks they thought interesting (see Appendix A). They could, for several lessons, work independently to compile some 'in-depth' research either on their own or with friends. It had to include evidence of appropriate reading, analysis and their own writing. This was the point when I had to have plenty of resources to hand. The school library helped with a box of assorted books, pictures and pamphlets. I brought in a further stock of books and mini-guides (individualised pointers to very specific questions, certain references to book pages and passages, graded and minimum targets to reach according to interest and ability). To provide a further thread I reminded them about earlier days of soldiering by looking at part of Roy Palmer's useful book (1977) of photos, pictures, ballads and memoirs reaching back to the eighteenth century. Finally, from an available range in the classroom we read a couple of war poems at the start of the next two lessons. Lessons then took on their own life with students engaged at tables, writing and reading, jotting and sketching, taping in the English Department's staff-room, browsing in the library or chatting to me about their next move.

By the end of the fifth or sixth week and with half-term approaching most students had achieved minimum targets: several different types of writing; a lot of talk in small units; looking, listening and reading into material which could engage them casually and/or quite consciously. At best it was becoming a respectable unity of experience and when John, for instance, had read Thomas Hardy's 'The Man He Killed' he could see that:

> The poet writes as though he doesn't know why he is in the war. He doesn't understand why he killed the enemy . . . he couldn't exactly find out why men do this in war and explains it as quaint and curious because there is no proper answer.

John's own war poem, though unspectacular, was full of empathy too, even though his treatment of a solitary death was apparently stark and detached:

> The gun barrel slid silently through the leaves,
> Its cold steel pointing in the direction
> Of the lone figure.
> The trigger squeezed easily in the socket.
> A shot rang out and the bullet slid home
> Into the flesh.
> He never moved again after he hit the forest floor.

What pleased me most was the acceptance that we could no longer talk easily or verge on the sensational aspects without sterner consideration of our terms of reference. Our thinking was changing through our changing language. It had become possible to speak in the same conversation of *Dad's Army*, a nine o'clock television news bulletin about mercenaries in Africa, Owen's 'Mental Cases', a television viewing of Kubrick's *Paths of Glory*, a Giles cartoon of prisoner-of-war life in the Second World War, and the rifle bayonet I used at home to poke the fire. The connections strengthened as the students faced outward realities with inward visions.

After the half-term break it was time to extend the studies and to consider what was different and special about war in the twentieth century. To introduce this and give some historical edge and persuasion to what might become a more demanding series of assignments, I played a graphic BBC Radio-Vision programme about trench warfare. We read the opening chapters of *All Quiet on the Western Front* together and I asked them to explain what they had learned about battle in 1914–18. They were surprised that Remarque should be writing sympathetically about Germans: the same Germans in the war comics?

The plan was to read the novel in serial form in three weeks of lessons and homeworks. Some girls were resistant, but on reaching the chapters about leave they saw that women were significant . . . and if they didn't appear to be, well, that raised all sorts of questions about females and war didn't it? Increasingly now I was trying to enlist the girls to provoke the boys about such subjects as heroism and duty, patriotism and pacifism, comradeship and physical combat. During these sessions over weeks seven, eight and nine the novel and the 1930 film version by Lewis Milestone (the whole year-group saw this and discussed it in deliberately planned small groups with some staff participation) were the focus as well as 'paired' poems from the Great War. Talk and writing grew around this. Stephen's poem was a typical response. It got close to the art-language of the time but also came near to a Second World War poet like Alun Lewis:

'Blood and Muck'

Rain. It always seemed to rain now.
I can hear it splashing off the steel helmets
And dripping off corrugated sheets of iron.
Grey skies lit by orange flashes on the horizon.
The rumbling of guns or was it thunder?
Our plan went wrong, the attack failed.
We, the dead and dying, are the only ones to tell the story.

The whistle of a misaimed shell is heard above.
Nearby it lands, casting foreign land about us.
The battle is gone and we are forgotten.
What of my family, will they know of my fate?
Will my child ever think of me? I don't know.
Is it a tear on my face, or is it just the rain –
Rain that runs into pads or pink-brown sludge
Around my slain comrades.

My comrades with whom I have laughed and cried,
Who have given reassuring words to those who need them.
They lie in ridiculous poses, all with the same face.
The face of the young dead.

I am to join them now, for I am dying.
To lie in the same pose, with the same look.
How the rain now falls, heavy with uncaring –
For me to die in the blood and muck.

Apart from poems and documentary, analysis and comprehension (I mean subtle forms of 'comprehending' through informal writing; not the grind of twenty questions set by the teacher), I wanted a further kind of substantial response. One of the possibilities amongst a wide choice of activities at this later stage was writing a series of war letters to and from Paul Baumer, the 'hero' of Remarque's novel. This demanded understanding of text and character and called for a consideration of language and tone in a more deliberate 'composition'.

Josie captured the tender side of Paul in a letter sent to his sister, Erna:

Tell mother I am well then her mind will be at rest. The trenches are not better, the wet and filth, the cold, clinging nights, and, most important, the food. Corned beef is our diet every day. I suppose the food situation is no better back at home, but still, we have to make the most of what we have got . . . Tell Mother nothing of this. I had to tell you my secret.

In another version of this letter Richard got Paul to recall the shell hole incident with the French soldier he had mortally wounded:

At the time it was me against him, my life against his. He didn't see me so I seized my chance. He was stricken so violently, three stab wounds to the chest. He lay there for hours dying in that filthy hole, rats crawling, seizing their chances of food.
   He may be considered the enemy by you but having killed him and looked at him I began to think – why did they not tell us . . . we are all the same, we all had families, so why, why this damned war?

When Philip wrote a long letter, again from Paul to Erna, his sympathy and insight was total:

Dear Erna, I have something I must tell you which is so disturbing . . . I can't keep it bottled up . . . We needed to discover just how strong the enemy position was manned . . . I crept forward until I found refuge in a shell hole. I peered up over the edge to see what was happening. I remember a machine gun spreading bullets across the cratered field. I had to keep low because it swept across from all directions leaving nowhere untouched . . . Shells crashed continuously and machine guns rattled an unbroken chain of sound . . . The thing that gets me really mad is that a high class officer sits in his nice clean uniform smoking his cigar while we do the fighting and kill for him. I bet half of them have never seen the enemy . . .

The First World War has been emphatically chronicled. There is no shortage of evidence. We listened to a recording of *Oh What a Lovely War*, to the sounds of real guns on a specialist record, to the BBC

Scapbook of the period. Now into our last two or three weeks it was time to come up to date. With less time to indulge than there had been with the Great War I now had to ensure that individuals could range over the last forty years quite randomly. A key poem, 'Vergissmeinnicht' by Keith Douglas, centred attention on the results of killing. That led to students dipping into a final 'box of bits': maybe a recent novel for youngsters like Robert Westall's *The Machine Gunners*; or the more political *The Real Life of Domingos Xavier*, a novel of Angola by J. L. Vieira; poems of protest about Vietnam; enough copies of *Twelve War Stories*, a useful selection covering the whole period under scrutiny. Guided to a particular reading and/or looking (I had a lot of modern war scenes in pictures and photos stuck on card and linked tasks on the reverse) students completed the term's programme or had the chance to redraft in the holiday. We didn't rule out the future possibilities for war: our very last lesson that term was on 'Your Attention Please' by Peter Porter and the cooler 'Defence', the war poem by Jon Silkin. Those who went on to read Graham Greene's *Discovery in the Woods* could ponder the possibilities of a post-nuclear war future.

Nuclear warfare is, of course, the most urgent area for classroom work. Given the time, I should have extended our studies here conspicuously. Apart from the familiar texts (for example, John Hersey's *Hiroshima*) and films (such as Peter Watkins' *The War Game*), there are now ample resources for those wishing to give it appropriate attention in their classrooms. The nuclear age is well served by its official propagandists, and pupils need to look hard at the language which disguises the true and fundamental issues. A useful starter for teachers and students is Arnold Wesker's essay, 'Words' (1974). A range of accessible poetry and fiction (especially 'science fiction') now makes this subject just as valid in the mainstream of English studies as it may be in historical, social or peace studies. The recent English Programme series called 'Power' is published as part of *Studio Scripts* (1981) edited by David Self and Andrew Bethel. Other useful references are *Adam's Ark* (1981) by Harold Hodgson, and Peter Kennard's *No Nuclear Weapons* (1981), for its associated and powerful visual images.

Looking back there were definite failings; I had not allowed enough breathing space for individuals to self-assess nor to clarify aims. Moreover, not everyone enjoyed or benefited from the study although most had, encouragingly, enjoyed it some of the time. There had been too much to teach, and too much time spent in direct teaching. I should have withdrawn and been less regulatory, allowing students to make their own choices. The final lessons were a dash.

The notable achievement was an adjustment of perception, and therefore of thought among the students. By the end they had grasped the inimical language of crucial war experiences, had contemplated seriously what Owen called 'the pity of war' and had grappled with their own consciences. They had begun to sense the momentousness of war in individual and public lives.

Gradually and accumulatively, through a process of exploration, description, and interpretations, the students gained a degree of critical insight. The literary and other art-work gave us the most exact and integrated views of the war experience. The intention, through talking, listening, looking and thinking, and by reading and writing, had been to secure connections between the individual student and the social world of 'war'. Art-language was an extension of that dialogue, part of the continuum of what is inside us (the personal) and what is outside us (the social).

Of course much of the lesson time was given to checking, motivating, guiding, informing, intervening, modifying, joking, chatting and so on. But the main challenge I tried to meet was the necessary incorporation of art-work into both cultural activity and into the life-contexts of the students. 'The experience of war' was medium and message; literature was part of our cultural exchange. It was never too ambitious to expect serious encounters between strenuous texts and not-so-innocent readers. Our dialogues did not start or end there anyway; novels, stories, poems, were all part of the arguments and conversations of the classroom. In this classroom work I had seen the literature as a central illumination of the known and knowable world; not in isolation, but as a living, connecting and penetrating force of human awareness. It is in this sense that 'art' meets the language and knowingness of the pupils. It is in this sense too that the really worthwhile art experiences (including the pupils' own works which approach the status of 'art') have a special meaning for us today; they can help to seal links between art and politics, between the experiences of individuals and the attitudes of their societies.

Bibliography

Battle Picture Weekly, 12 April 1975 (IPC Magazines)
HERSEY, J. (1969) *Hiroshima* (Penguin)
HODGSON, H. (1981) *Adam's Ark* (Macmillan)
KENNARD, P. (1981) *No Nuclear Weapons* (Campaign for Nuclear Disarmament/Pluto Press)
PACKWOOD, C. Unpublished memoirs.
PALMER, R. (1977) *The Rambling Soldier* (Penguin)
ROSEN, H. (1981) 'Neither Bleak House nor Liberty Hall' (University of London, Institute of Education)
SELF, D. and BETHEL, E. (ed.) (1981) *Studio Scripts* (Hutchinson/Thames)
THOMAS, D. (1977) *Battle Art: Images of War* (Phaidon)
VYGOTSKY, L. S. (1962) *Thought and Language* (MIT Press)
WESKER, A. (1974) *Words* (Writers and Readers)
WILLIAMS, R. (1958) *Culture and Society* (Chatto)
WILLIAMS, R. (1980) *Politics and Letters* (New Left Books)

Appendix A: CSE English Topic (Copy to each pupil)
The Experience of War

As well as reading *The Red Badge of Courage, All Quiet on the Western Front*, a variety of poems and memoirs, you should attempt one of the following subjects and its required study:

1   **A War Anthology** Make your own personal comment by collecting, arranging and writing about poems, prose, pictures, whose subject is war. Refer to the Reading List and look also at art and photography by Sidney Nolan, Keith Douglas, Robert Capa, Picasso, Goya, Don McCullin.

2   How were the following poets killed in war? Edward Thomas, Wilfred Owen, Isaac Rosenberg, Keith Douglas, Alun Lewis, Sidney Keyes. Copy one poem and add your own comments about it.

3   Try to see some of the best war films: *All Quiet on the Western Front; King and Country; The Way to the Stars; The Red Badge of Courage; The Men.* Write a review of *one* or more of these (or another you have seen) showing its meaning and attitudes. (When you are older try to see *The War Game* by Pete Watkins: a devastating film about what would happen if a nuclear attack struck this country. An updated version is now being prepared.)

4   Read 'What to do when the Sirens start' and 'Your Attention Please'. What are the essential differences between the 'real' advice and the poem which envisages a nuclear attack? Imagine *you* are involved in one of these air raids. Describe what happens as vividly as you can. This can be a poem but might be more realistic as a documentary re-telling.

5   Read the poems by Henry Reed: 'Naming of Parts' and 'Judging Distances'. By referring closely to the poems illustrate the purpose of the poet here. Find out how soldiers are drilled and trained (today especially; ask a local cadet) and what kinds of enticement/ propaganda are used to obtain recruits.

6   Watch some current television programmes dealing with war as a background: *London Belongs to Me; It ain't arf ot Mum; Dad's Army; Secret Army.* Write about any of these, trying to explain their basic appeal today. Interview anyone who *actually* lived through one of those kinds of situations (close relations, neighbours). Reveal *their* attitudes.

7   Read any one of the books from the Reading List and then write a review expressing your views about its appeal: the kind of experience, the language and attitudes, the effect it now has.

8   Read *Dooley is a Traitor* by James Michie and research into the subject of Conscientious Objectors. What are your views about this

and what is today called 'pacifism'? (Discuss this difficult subject with others.)

9 Read and look at some war comics and the article 'Why Are Children So Fascinated By War?'.

Then try to analyse the appeal and contents of such material: include the **language** and **attitudes**; the **morality**; the possible **effects** on readers.

10 Read the Letters in *Impact One*, pages 96–9, and the letter explaining Robert Graves' 'death' in *Goodbye to All That*. Put yourself imaginatively in the place of a soldier and write your letter to either your sweetheart, or your wife and family, or your parents.

11 Read any of the following 'paired' poems and compare them in **style, emotional appeal** (what feelings they evoke and emphasise), and general **effect.**
R. Brooke, 'The Soldier' and W. Owen, 'The Sentry'.
W. Wordsworth, 'Character of the Happy Warrior' and H. Read, 'The Happy Warrior'.
L. Binyon, 'For the Fallen' and W. Owen, 'Dulce et Decorum Est'.
R. Brooke, 'Peace' and W. Owen, 'Disabled'.

12 Choose any one of the following experiences and write in your own way about *one* (for example, poetry; comment; story; script).
(a) An atomic bomb explosion seen from a safe distance (ask for a photo).
(b) An imaginary meeting between two enemies in battle (for example, as ghosts, in 'Strange Meeting' by W. Owen).
(c) An imaginary meeting of two ex-soldiers (former enemies) in peacetime.
(d) The thoughts of a soldier who revisits the scene of battle some years later.
(e) By identifying with a soldier 'at the front' describe one of the following:
(i) Waiting for the Attack; (ii) Night; (iii) The Survivor; (iv) The Coward; (v) Leaving for the Front; (vi) On Leave; (vii) The Raid; (viii) Sentry Duty.
(f) An imagined 'domestic' conversation at 'home'; for example in the London Underground during an air-raid; discussing war news.

13 Write a careful and detailed study of the poem 'Defence' by Jon Silkin. Explain it sentence by sentence. Consider the attitude of the poet. What does he want us to think and feel when we have read it? How successful is he? Try writing your own poem of protest about nuclear war. (See your teacher for further information on this subject.)

14 Write a study of 'Women and War'. Look closely at the way women

are expected to behave in wartime and at their actual attitudes and experiences. Again obtain information from your teacher but also talk to women who have experienced war, perhaps your grandmother. Investigate literature about and by women on this subject.

Appendix B: Resources and Sources for the Teacher

Books

ADAMS, A. (ed.) (1975) *War* (Pergamon)

CATTON, B. (1968) *The American Civil War* (Penguin)

CRANE, S. (1895) *The Red Badge of Courage* (Hutchinson Educational, 1964)

DEIGHTON, L. (1978) *Bomber* (Panther)

DEIGHTON, L. (1979) *Fighter* (Panther)

DEIGHTON, L. (1981) *Blitzkreig* (Panther)

DOUGLAS, K. (1964) *Selected Poems* (Faber)

DOUGLAS, K. (1969) *From Alamain to Zem Zem* (Penguin)

FUSSELL, P. (1977) *The Great War and Modern Memory* (Oxford University Press)

GARDNER, B. (ed.) (1974) *Up The Line to Death* – Poetry Anthology (Methuen)

GARDNER, B. (ed.) (1976) *The Terrible Rain* – Poetry Anthology (Methuen)

HALSON, G. (ed.) (1980) *Twelve War Stories* (Longman Imprint)

HARRISON, T. (1978) *Living Through the Blitz* (Penguin)

HELLER, J. (1962) *Catch 22* (Cape)

HERSEY, J. (1969) *Hiroshima* (Penguin)

JUNGK, R. (1968) *Children of the Ashes* (Penguin)

MAILER, N. (1958) *The Naked and the Dead* (Panther)

NYISZLI, M. (1964) *Auschwitz* (Panther)

OWEN, W. (1963) *Collected Poems* (Chatto)

PALMER, R. (ed.) (1977) *The Rambling Soldier* (Penguin)

PARSONS, I. (ed.) (1978) *Men Who March Away* (Chatto)

REMARQUE, E. (1929) *All Quiet on the Western Front* (Heinemann Windmill, 1973)

ROSENBERG, I. (1975) *Word and Image* (National Book League, exhibition catalogue)

ROTHBERG, A. (1973) *Eyewitness History of World War Two* (Bantam)

SNYDER, L. (1955) *Fifty Major Documents of the Twentieth Century* (Anvil)

SUMMERFIELD, G. (ed.) (1968) *Voices, The Third Book* (Penguin)

THOMAS, D. (1977) *Battle Art/Images of War* (Phaidon)

WHITE, D. (1976) 'Why Are Children So Fascinated By War?' in *New Society*, 11 November, pages 295–7

WINTER, D. (1979) *Death's Men* (Penguin)

Materials for the classroom

Print Resources

Class Sets of: *The Red Badge of Courage,*
All Quiet on the Western Front,
Twelve War Stories.

Short Story Sets of: *An Occurrence at Owl Creek Bridge,*
The Upturned Face,
One of the Missing.

Sets of various war comics, magazines and booklets.
Various facsimiles of Second World War editions of the *Daily Mail.*
War Letters published and private.
Extracts from *The Rambling Soldier.*
The following poems:

R. BROOKE, 'The Soldier', 'Peace';
W. OWEN, 'The Sentry', 'Dulce Et Decorum Est', 'Disabled', 'Mental Cases';
W. WORDSWORTH, 'Character of the Happy Warrior';
H. READ, 'The Happy Warrior';
I. ROSENBERG, 'Dead Man's Dump', 'Lice Killing';
S. SASSOON, 'In the Pink';
K. DOUGLAS, 'Vergissmeinnicht', 'How to Kill'.

Second World War air raid instructions.
1980 Government pamphlet *Protect and Survive.*

Visual Resources

A large reproduction of Picasso's painting 'Guernica'.
A large selection of war photos taken from newspapers and magazines.
A Radio-vision programme from the BBC on the First World War.
Lewis Milestone's film of *All Quiet on the Western Front* available from: MCA Films, Kingston Road, Merton Park, London SW19
Dennis Sander's film *A Time Out of War* available from: Connoisseur Films Ltd, 167 Oxford Street, London W1.
Robert Enrico's film of *An Occurrence at Owl Creek Bridge* available from: Connoisseur Films Ltd, 167 Oxford Street, London W1.
(The film is actually called *Incident at Owl Creek.*)

Recordings

Joan Littlewood's 'Oh What a Lovely War', (Decca) SPA 27
'The Voice of Richard Dimbleby', (MFP) 1087
'What Passing Bell', (Argo) RG 385
'BBC Scrapbook for 1914', (Fontana) 493 014 FDL
'Voices Book Three', Record Two DA 96

10 Creative Responses in the Sixth Form

John Brown and Terry Gifford

Introduction

As the summit of English studies in school, why is 'A' level English often so disappointing? It promises well, with major writers at its centre; but the influence of the examination system has promoted narrow forms of assessment which have little, if any, room for students' creativity and which recognise only a severely limited kind of writing. It is a sad irony that on a course which is so art-centred the timed critical essay should have the monopoly.

What kind of influence does that specialised form of writing have on the way students read and respond to books? Is there a danger that analysis and exegesis can function independently of a student's felt response? In the following pages we shall offer practical suggestions for helping to develop a student's responsiveness and understanding, and ways of linking books and other forms of art. The suggestions are largely based on work either completed or in progress in a comprehensive school on a council estate in North Sheffield.

We shall describe ways of working which encourage students to have confidence in their engagement with a book by admitting a wider range of response, including creative work (as in the sections on poetry and documentary). We briefly touch upon the need to consider stages of learning in a course, with ideas for individual and group activities. In a section on *The Grapes of Wrath* we suggest ways in which the cultural context of a work of art can inform judgement and extend the sympathies through other art-forms. Our contention is that the wide range of teaching techniques and creative modes of work used lower down the school should enhance the development of a fully involved, individually critical engagement with a text in the Sixth Form. It is heartening that much of what we describe has been stimulated by now established alternative 'A' level syllabuses which move beyond the conceptions of English underlying the traditional forms of assessment (such new schemes have been developed, for example, by the Associated Examining Board (AEB) and the Joint Matriculation Board (JMB). See the appendix to this chapter, page 150).

Induction and Beyond: Group Engagements with Poetry

Students need to have time to find their own way into a text, to make the text their own in some sense, before the rigours of a teacher-led class discussion. As Peter Clough has described in his chapter on classroom talk, small group work can provide the support and questioning necessary for tentative explorations. The degree of structure and the direction of its focus in the activities described below must be seen in relation to the stages of learning for which they were devised, whether it be the teaching or discovering of a particular concept, exploration of an area of experience, coming at a set text through juxtaposition with others, or initiation into the experience of group work itself.

An induction session for Fifth Formers about to join the Sixth Form was arranged, which aimed to indicate something of the range of activities in Sixth Form English, and to begin to forge working relationships through an exploration of the central idea in Ted Hughes' *Crow* poem 'Lineage'. A part of the Genesis creation story, followed by a Biblical lineage, was read to the class. Then, in groups of three, students were given an envelope containing the separate lines of the Hughes poem. Each group was asked to arrange the lines into a sequence, to create stanza spaces as necessary, and to glue this sequence on to a sheet of paper. The groups gave a choral reading of their version to the class. Then each member of the group was asked to select one line from their sequence on to which to add the word 'because' and complete as a sentence. The class then listened to a recording of Hughes reading his poem 'Lineage', were given a copy, and again asked to add 'because' to one line each in order to complete a sentence. Next, groups of six were formed and asked to produce a lineage poem of twelve lines, by the process of each member contributing one line and passing the poem on until it had been round the group twice. Finally individuals were asked to tell, in a poem of their own, the lineage story of an object or creature from its earliest form, perhaps through some metamorphosis, to its present condition.

Later work on *Crow* began with groups preparing readings of the following six poems for a ritualised class performance: 'Lineage', 'Examination at the Womb-door', 'Crow's First Lesson', 'Crow Tyrannosauros', 'Crow and the Sea', and 'How Water Began to Play'. This selection provides a narrative framework through some of the best poems in the book. Work progressed to consider two questions: 'Of what story might these songs be the fragments?' and 'Write the anthropologist's report on the tribe which tells the story of *Crow*. What are their qualities?' Whilst striking at the heart of what *Crow* is about through creative work on the first question, the second question requires analysis and judgement.

Similar kinds of activities were devised as preparation for class discussion of earlier Hughes poems which were in the set text. These ranged from open-ended explorations to activities which drew attention to a particular area of experience or way of reading a poem. Three poems concerning death were given to the students: 'Dulce Et Decorum Est' by Owen, 'Vergissmeinnicht' by Keith Douglas, and Hughes' 'The Green Wolf'. Students were asked to place the three poems in an order or sequence before explaining their criteria by quotation. The effect of this is to have some comparative responses to each author's treatment of death brought to a discussion, which can then clarify each individual's readings of the poems from there.

In order to introduce a sense of the writer's stance towards subject matter a more structured and deliberately narrow activity was based on Lawrence's 'Fish' and Hughes' 'Pike'. Students were asked to use a scale in which -10 represented an extreme of 'subjectivity', the author completely identifying with his subject matter, and $+10$ represented the opposite extreme of 'objectivity', in which the author is a detached observer of his subject matter. Pairs of students were asked to give each poem a score on this scale. The average results of -7 for 'Fish' and $+4$ for 'Pike' are not in themselves as important as the perception of this dimension in the poems. The importance of the writer's stance to the achievement of each poem needs evaluating in discussion, which is the better for the concept having been used rather than externally produced.

Our last example of group engagement with poetry is not as a starting point for response but provides an opportunity for taking stock in the process of sorting out what is actually going on in the head of Hamlet. We had been reading *Hamlet* with some attempt to sense the dramatic tension in Hamlet's contributions in the early scenes. We had just read the 'To be or not to be' soliloquy, and needed to pause to consider the nature of Hamlet's self-questioning before the turning-point of the play scene. Students were given copies of three poems: 'I Am' by John Clare, 'I Am Vertical' by Sylvia Plath, and 'Wodwo' by Ted Hughes. In small groups students were asked to find any links between these poems and Hamlet's state of mind at this point in the play. They were given a big sheet of card and felt-tipped pens of two colours, as they were asked to show visually the relationship between these texts for a new reader of them. This card was to act as a guide for such a reader and could utilise arrows, quotations, annotations, and titles. One of the results is shown on p. 142, and although it is shorthand for the results of group discussion it does represent a coherent summary of the essential qualities of the poetry as it relates to Hamlet's state of mind. The placing of Clare's melodious lines beside the frenzied logic of Hamlet provides the material for further discussion of Hamlet's fear of, and flirtation with, self-deception. Isn't Sylvia Plath's 'useful' a false concept as much as the Wodwo's casual assumption that he is 'the exact centre'? Further questions arise out of the student's own consideration, selection and presentation, but can be followed through in the knowledge that an engagement of some quality has already taken place.

Exploring the Art of Documentary

A well-chosen non-fiction book is worth an early place on an 'A' level course because of its likely accessibility, and because it can lead to some simple practical investigations by students. Orwell's *The Road to Wigan*

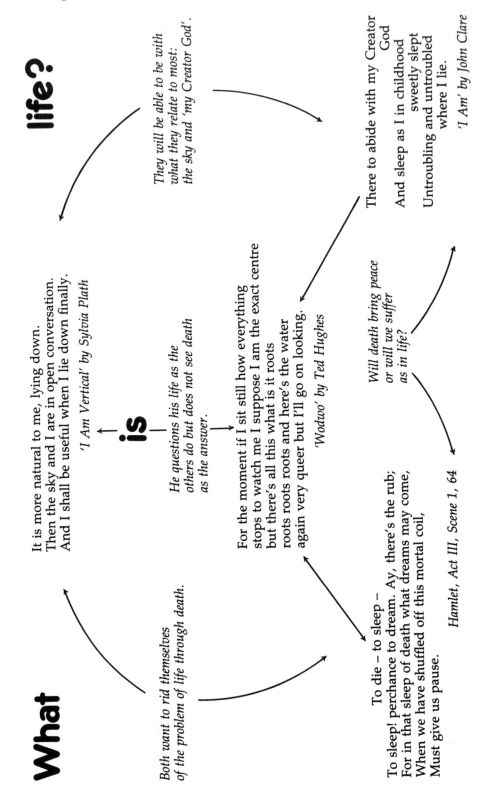

life?

They will be able to be with
what they relate to most:
the sky and 'my Creator God'.

There to abide with my Creator
God
And sleep as I in childhood
sweetly slept
Untroubling and untroubled
where I lie.
'I Am' by John Clare

It is more natural to me, lying down.
Then the sky and I are in open conversation.
And I shall be useful when I lie down finally.
'I Am Vertical' by Sylvia Plath

is

He questions his life as the
others do but does not see death
as the answer.

For the moment if I sit still how everything
stops to watch me I suppose I am the exact centre
but there's all this what is it roots
roots roots roots and here's the water
again very queer but I'll go on looking.
'Wodwo' by Ted Hughes

Will death bring peace
or will we suffer
as in life?

What

Both want to rid themselves
of the problem of life through death.

To die – to sleep –
To sleep! perchance to dream. Ay, there's the rub;
For in that sleep of death what dreams may come,
When we have shuffled off this mortal coil,
Must give us pause.
Hamlet, Act III, Scene 1, 64

Pier is a seminal choice on a syllabus, both as a key book from the pioneering days of documentary in the 1930s and in raising many of the basic issues about the art of documentary.

At a first reading many students may take Orwell's book as the kind that seems to offer empirical evidence of such a nature as to render dispute unlikely. However, on closer study, the reader will almost certainly want to know to what extent he can trust the artist's integrity.

The film-maker Grierson defined documentary as 'the creative treatment of actuality'; both in the process of gathering the material and in editing and selecting for the final draft the individual writer or maker of documentary will have his own bias and criteria. Moreover, whenever language is used to describe 'actuality', by its very nature it confers a degree of disjunction from reality that offers opportunity for deception. Bernard Harrison's introduction warns that art ought not to be confused with propaganda; how, then, can students be helped to discover these kinds of problems for themselves?

One obvious starting point is to look at one of the first published documentaries, Defoe's *Journal of the Plague Year*, which was published in 1722 about events in London in 1665, when its author was only four years old. The book claims to record 'observations . . . of the most remarkable occurrences written by a citizen who continued all the while in London', and the growing reading public at the time seems to have accepted this reconstructed eye-witness account. A close look at the *Journal* will offer significant clues as to how a writer captures this trust – by its detailed graphic narrative, its use of statistics, its personal asides and its dramatised dialogues. Students can be invited to say how far they think Defoe is a reliable reporter by comparison with parts of Cobbett's *Rural Rides*. It is important for students to meet committed thinkers from earlier periods, whose treatment of strong social, moral and political purposes may be compared with Orwell.

At this stage, students can be shown some of the photographs from the 1930s, particularly those of Bill Brandt. His book, *The English at Home* appeared in 1936, a year before Orwell's, when Brandt had decided to concentrate on reportage and documentary; it contains photographs of miners, both at work and at home. Another resource are the Mass Observation archives, but these are more selective because the aim of that group was to be more 'scientific'. Compared to Orwell's description of the Lancashire slums, the Mass Observation photographs of Bolton by Humphrey Spender seem to avoid those harsh conditions.

Students can now be asked to make their own short documentaries, in groups, ideally armed with cameras and tape recorders. Their aim is to try to record actuality, with no more specific purpose declared, since the process of editing will then become very revealing. Clearly photographs impose their own limited framework on reality, and when tapes are transcribed and edited then the resulting tape/slide programme will inevitably be a very selective presentation of what students actually witnessed on location, especially if one student in each group has acted as observer during the whole operation. It may be possible, using the same basic material, but by selecting different sequences of slides and tape, or by omitting certain images and sounds, to produce two or three different documentaries. The shock of recognition experienced by the students, gained during the process of making, can give an impetus to study of social, moral and political aspects of art; and practical investigations of this kind are well worth giving time to.

On returning to Orwell, two sections of the book can be looked at closely: that which records the author's first visit underground to a pit, and some later pages about scrambling for coal. Earlier drafts of these pages are to be found in 'Diary of the Road to Wigan Pier' (in *Collected Essays, Journals and Letters*, Vol. I, 1968), and it is revealing to make a detailed comparison of tone, presentation and selection of material. The changes in the text show Orwell's awareness of his audience who were, in the first place, members of the Left Book Club.

It is also useful to compare Orwell's attitude to miners, remembering that he was from a middle-class background, to that of D. H. Lawrence in 'Nottingham and the Mining Country' and B. L. Coombes, a Welsh miner, in his autobiography *These Poor Hands*. A photo-narrative about Coombes appeared in *Picture Post* (4 January 1941); Henry Moore's distinguished drawings of miners at work are a further valuable source. There are more recent reports on mining to look at – *Weekend at Dimlock* by C. Sigal (1960), and a collection of reminiscences by miners themselves, *Essays from the Yorkshire Coalfield* (published by the University of Sheffield, 1979). Having a range of attitudes to consider makes it easier for students to judge whether Orwell indulges in a form of hero worship of working men at times.

Essential reading at this stage is Orwell's essay 'Why I Write', since there he declares his political commitment in all his writing since 1936, the year before he wrote *The Road to Wigan Pier*. A comparison with Grierson's classic film *Drifters*, which is still available for hire, offers another perspective, since the dignified images of fishermen are similar in spirit and intention to the word pictures of miners by Orwell.

Yet further work can be linked to some of Orwell's other documentary type essays and books – 'Shooting an Elephant', 'How the Poor Die', *Down and Out in Paris and London* and *Homage to Catalonia*. By then students may have come to judge for themselves Orwell's integrity and achievement as a committed writer. Such delicate questions cannot be resolved in the instant and final form of a homework's essay. Truly personal judgements of tone can be sharpened by direct experience of artistic choices when the work of several artists is seen fresh from the exercise of those choices in practical explorations of the art of documentary.

Response to Drama in Performance

It is a commonly argued point that drama texts should be regarded as printed intentions for live effects in performance, and the study of plays through some sort of dramatic exploration by students' own drama work is commonly advocated. For English students this is usually intended to help them answer examination questions about the imagined dramatic possibilities of the printed text. The alternative AEB and JMB syllabuses give provision in their coursework element for written responses to live performances. Again this is often claimed to be important in drama study on English courses, but the evidence is rarely produced for the kind of perceptions that can be gained from the linked study of text and performance.

Maria had read *Hamlet* with her class as a first experience of Shakespeare in the Lower Sixth; she had been involved in improvisations, scene performances, and discussions that had focused on the problems and insights presented to an audience by the unfolding of the play. After seeing a performance at Stratford in her second term Maria wrote in her review of that performance:

> The performance of Hamlet was interesting and sensitive, something reading the play does not always create. Hamlet's character was portrayed with understanding, his madness being given a purpose, to show the true life of the court, yet as in most human situations, showing times when it got out of control. The most realistic element of this performance was not only the perceptive manner Hamlet was given but the fact that during and after the performance his character could not be clearly assessed or defined. Like a living being he was too deep and complexed (*sic*) a character to be drawn out with mere words.

This may be escaping some complexities at this stage, yet whilst it is struggling with a sense of the dramatic enigma of Hamlet's character there is a clear view of Hamlet's role in the whole drama, 'his madness being given a purpose'.

Ashley, on the other hand, in reviewing a performance of *The Caucasian Chalk Circle*, again after prior reading and discussion of the text, was quite specific about the nature of the complexities of the character of Azdak:

> The production does not show Azdak's contradictions well. Nicky Henson, who played Azdak (at Sheffield), seems constantly to indulge the character's senses, without showing how mentally alert Azdak is. Azdak is not shocking to the audience because Henson assumes that his contradictions are simply those of a corrupt man. Azdak's apparent corruptness, however, is rational and based on logic. He is, therefore, parodying the corrupt nature of the court system. It is not until the trial involving Grusha that the audience truly sees the dominance of Azdak's shrewdness over Grusha's simple goodness.

This sense of measuring up an actor's or a director's interpretation of the same text read earlier by the student can lead to suggestions for improvement in dramatic effects that are sharp, clear and physical in their expression of an intellectual perception. At the time of writing her first account, Celestine did not know about Brecht's use of masks for the soldiers in his original production of *The Caucasian Chalk Circle*:

In order to create the atmosphere of fear and tension on stage, and conveying the same feeling of fear which I felt while reading the play, the director should have portrayed the iron shirts wearing a black mask, shaped like a dome, smooth, with no indentations representing a mouth or ears. The back and front should have been indistinguishable so that the mask is transporting (*sic*) the image that the iron shirts have no feeling or loyalty.

In the theatre, 'Truth is concrete' is Brecht's famous motto. It must be said that in getting students to write about its enactment, rather than as a book only, practice is an advantage, and the focus of discussion on the physical and contextual nature of meaning in theatre is also necessary. We saw a play and reviewed its performance once each term, not confining ourselves to the productions of texts of which we had copies, but also choosing new plays at our local studio theatre that made full use of the vibrant liveness of performance, and of course, some that didn't!

In order to achieve the subtle yet clear understanding of Azdak's character that Ashley's paragraph shows, it is necessary to accept the conditions of turmoil in which Azdak attempts to survive. Celestine's expression of the Ironshirts' lack of 'feeling or loyalty' that creates these conditions takes the form of a vivid practical image. Like Ashley she writes with a thoughtful, felt understanding of the nature of meaning in dramatic performance.

Text and context – The Grapes of Wrath

The uncelebrated dramas of our students' own lives in the community are a resource for learning that is traditionally neglected most in the Sixth Form. Yet the concept of 'relevance' in relation to a text like *The Grapes of Wrath* can only be accurately applied if attention is paid as much to differences as to similarities with contemporary family life, unemployment and social change. The slide/tape sequence, '*Grapes of Wrath* and the 1930s' is an American production (EAV Inc) which brings together the classic photographs of the period, Woody Guthrie's songs, readings from the novel and an informative commentary on the economic background to the movement of migrant workers from the Mid West during the 1930s. This combination of art-forms makes the unfolding of the historical story a powerful experience in its own right. As an introduction to a study of the novel the combination of modes helps an understanding of economic and social processes to be formed in a way that is not separated from the authentic quality and response to the experience in the lives of people themselves.

We began with Part II of the sequence which deals with the wider economic and political perspectives, making notes at the second running of it so that the historical processes could be identified. An important element in the approach of this sequence is that these processes are seen to be the dynamics of the policies and motivations of men, as seen all the time in the photographs. This is an important perception to bring to a discussion of the extent to which Steinbeck reifies 'the Banks' in the novel. When we ran Part I of the sequence the focus of attention was on the direct experiences of the farmers and migrants. After a first run-through of sound and photographs the photographs alone were discussed in terms of the emotions revealed in the subjects and the stance taken by the photographers. This led to questions about pride and dignity in relation to poverty. At the end of this discussion of the photographs students were asked to write in note form all they could about the actual experience of dispossession, unemployment and poverty in America in the 1930s from the evidence of the songs, novel extracts and tape commentary as well as the photographs. Drawing from these notes they were then asked to devise questions for an interview with a person at present unemployed, in order to discover differences and similarities in the experience and responses to it among their family, friends or neighbours today.

When the students returned with the results of their interviews attention was turned to the Woody Guthrie songs on the tape. Their form was discussed and the sources of the tunes discovered. Students were then asked to use the results of their interviews to write a song that would be a contemporary English equivalent to Guthrie's songs of the 1930s in America. To the tune of 'To Be A Sheffield Grinder' from the play *The Stirrings in Sheffield on Saturday Night*, Jane's song began:

'Ballad for the Unemployed'

To be unemployed in Britain
  it is no easy trade,
No hope for long-time jobless
  whose ideals have frayed,
No hope for all the people
  whose work they cannot find,
It's alright for the miners
  they have an axe to grind.

It's hard for all those people
  to look you in the face,
But don't you employ someone
  to come and take their place.
Remember they have feelings
  although they're hard to find;
Humiliated dole queues
  where all their names are signed.

Though people think you're lazy
  What else is there to do?
What else is there to offer?
  There's no jobs to go to
Your family and friends reject you
  they say you cause them shame
But one day in the future
  they may end up the same.

The tone of bitterness and frustration that expresses the detail ('humiliated dole queues') and trapped sense ('What else is there to do?') came to a head in the final lines quoted here. The obvious authenticity derived from the interview has found witty form in a parody of a popular local song about work.

By the time we began reading and discussing the novel itself Joe Klein's biography of Woody Guthrie (1981) was circulating; the visual ground had been prepared for our visit to John Ford's film of the novel at a later stage; some historical information had been noted to put alongside Steinbeck's political analysis; and most important, some engagement had been made with the nature of experiences of people like the Joads through other art-forms. The obvious strain and sense of indignity shown through the faces in the photographs, the last remnants of pride in the loaded cars of the migrants, the bitterness in the songs of Woody Guthrie, and making an articulation of our contemporary experiences of loss of work, all made the relevance of Steinbeck's novel obvious before we read it.

It is perhaps worth adding that in helping students to make a personal response to the novel at a first reading much use was made of students' personal reading diaries in the way suggested by David Jackson in *English in Education* (1979). Students were asked to read a section of the novel and then record in their diaries their immediate thoughts about it to bring to a class discussion or group work on that section of the book. Any class discussion thus began from points that interested or puzzled the students at first acquaintance; it then moved into areas that the teacher felt to be important if they had not been discussed already.

The diary is the place where early connections are made between the reader and the text, where the suggestions of the text are sorted out in relation to the reader's experience. Christine's comments on Chapter 19 in her reading diary *after* a class discussion represent a more reflective stage of evaluation of the text that is moving beyond a first engagement:

> Steinbeck realises that the stage is set for revolt, and assumes that it will come one day. He seems sure that he is right, and indeed the seeds of revolt are certainly present and growing, but, in the end, is he biased? Can the people really overcome their oppression? He sees from the inside as his writing of conversation shows. But the revolution is *not* inevitable. The poverty is short term, not long term as in other countries where revolution occurred. It seems to be wishful thinking on Steinbeck's part – wish for an uprising.

In our emphasis in this chapter on personal engagement, stages of learning, the opening of the sympathies by integrating art-forms in a way that does not truncate students' own creativity, we have not been arguing for an emotional identification that is separate from critical judgement. In this section for example our treating the matter of relevance as more than simple parallels has perhaps led to this sharply perceptive evaluation in Christine's diary. Certainly she needs to develop this response in a more considered statement by referring to Steinbeck's use of language in the text. Certainly, too, further questions remain. How far can our use of worksheets of detailed questions, related to key passages of the novel, help to sustain alert and felt response through to the final examination? To what extent can the problems of the assessment of students' own creative work be met by agreement trials for teachers, together with examiners, considering through actual examples the balances between suggestion and clarity, complexity and accuracy, experimentation and communication? The answers to questions such as these are urgently needed if our teaching in the Sixth Form is to allow as much for the wholeness of the growing person as for the wholeness of fully formed art. And in the end, of course, these must go together; since art, like language, can live only through those who use, and thereby continuously renew, art and language.

References

BRANDT, B. (1936) *The English at Home* (Batsford)

BRECHT, B. (1966) 'The Caucasian Chalk Circle' in *Parables for the Theatre* (Penguin)

COBBETT, W. (1830) *Rural Rides* (Penguin, 1967)

COOMBES, B. L. (1939) *These Poor Hands* (Gallanz)

DEFOE, D. (1722) *Journal of the Plague Year* (Penguin, 1966)

EAV INC. 'The Grapes of Wrath and the 1930s' slide/tape sequence R2 170 (Mary Glasgow Publications)

J. GRIERSON's film *Drifters* (1929) available from BFI, Central Film Library, 81 Dean Street, London, W1V 6AA

HARDY, F. (1979) *Grierson on Documentary* (Faber)

HUGHES, T. (1970) *Crow* (Faber)

KLEIN, J. (1981) *Woody Guthrie: a Biography* (Faber)

LAWRENCE, D. H. 'Nottingham and the Mining Country' in *Selected Essays* (Penguin, 1950)

MACFARLANE, J. (ed.) (1979) *Essays from the Yorkshire Coalfield* (University of Sheffield)

ORWELL, G. (1933) *Down and Out in Paris and London* (Penguin, 1962)
   (1938) *Homage to Catalonia* (Penguin, 1969)
   (1937) *The Road to Wigan Pier* (Penguin, 1962)
   (1961) 'Why I Write', 'Shooting an Elephant' and 'How the Poor Die' in *Collected Essays* (Mercury)
   (1968) 'Diary of the Road to Wigan Pier' in *The Collected Essays, Journals and Letters*, Vol. I (Secker)

SHAKESPEARE, W. *Hamlet*

SIGAL, C. (1960) *Weekend in Dimlock* (Secker)

SPENDER, H. photographs in *Camera Workshop* No. 11 (Mass Observation Issue) and (1982) *Worktown People* (Falling Wall Press)

STEINBECK, J. (1939) *The Grapes of Wrath* (Penguin, 1951)

Bibliography

CRAIG, D. and HEINEMANN, M., (1976) *Experiments in English Teaching* (Arnold)

DIXON, J. *et al.* (1979) *Education 16–19: The role of English and Communication* (Macmillan)

DIXON, J. and ROBERTS, N. (1978) 'Towards Changes at A Level' in *The Use of English*, Volume 29, No. 2

GILL, R. and JACKSON, D. (1980) 'Students Articulating their Response to Literature' in *Schools Council English 16–19 Project Booklet No. 9*

HARDING, D. W. (1977) 'Feeling Comprehension' in *The Cool Web* (ed.) MEEK, M. *et al.* (Bodley Head)

HORNER, S. and ALLEN, D. (1980) 'A Bang or a Whimper – A New 'A' Level Syllabus', in *English in Education*, Volume 14, No. 2

JACKSON, D. (1979) 'A Sixth Form Approach To Seamus Heaney' in *English in Education*, Volume 13, No. 3.

LEAVIS, F. R. (1977) *The Living Principle* (Chatto)

NEWTON, J. M. (1971) 'Literary Criticism, Universities, Murder', in *The Cambridge Quarterly*, Volume 5, No. 4.

POTTER, S. (1937) *The Muse in Chains* (Cape)

STANTON, M. (1980) 'Art Exists to Make the Stone Stoney', in *English in Education*, Volume 14, No. 3.

WITKIN, R. (1974) *The Intelligence of Feeling* (Heinemann)

Appendix: Two examples of Alternative 'A' level Schemes

(The information given below is reproduced by kind permission of Bill Greenwell and NATE Publications Committee, from NATE Examinations Booklet No. 4, *Alternatives at 'A' level*. This booklet contains a description of all current 'alternative' syllabuses and is issued free to NATE members.)

1 *AEB* (753)

Since 1977 (i.e. the first examination was taken in 1979), the AEB have offered an English syllabus which is almost wholly different from the traditional 652 syllabus they offer (the only crossover occurs in the precise selection of poets from one modern anthology). There are now 5 regional consortia, where there were at first 4; and there are now over 1000 candidates.

There are a number of innovations. There are 3 components of assessment: one practical criticism paper, to which there is an anthology of poetry attached; a set-books paper (Shakespeare; long poem; play; novel); and a 'component of internally assessed coursework'. Each component carries one third of the final marks. The 2 final papers allow for texts – which may be reasonably annotated – to be taken into the examination; the coursework is based on 9 pieces of work, consisting of 8 pieces of about 850 – 1000 words and an extended essay of about 3000 – 4000 words.

The coursework pieces must reflect the study of at least 6 texts, selected by the teachers and approved by the moderator; the extended essay must include evidence of study of at least one other text, although it may be based entirely on a selection made by the student and approved by the moderator. Of the 6 coursework texts, one must be non-fiction, and another a Shakespeare play. Two of the 8 shorter coursework pieces *must* be completed during the first year of the course.

After a successful initial experimental trial of 3 years, the scheme was approved in 1980 to continue for a further 3 years. A decision to make the scheme 'official' from 1983 onwards has now been taken.

Breakdown of assessment		%
Paper 1	Practical criticism (poetry)	11.1
	Practical criticism (prose)	11.1
	Poetry anthology	11.1
Paper 2	Shakespeare	8.3
	Long Poem	8.3
	Novel	8.3
	Play	8.3
Coursework	8 pieces of work approx. 1000 words	22.2
	Extended essay	11.1
		100.0

Comments and notes

1   The marginal annotation allowed on the texts to be taken into the final examination is unique; all others insist on 'plain texts'.

2   Both of the 3-hour final papers are extended by 15 minutes' *reading time*, since the nature of the examination means that far greater stress is laid on close textual commentary on selected passages, and far less on answering 'global questions'. See the passage later on open book examinations.

3   An exception is made in the novel's case. This cannot be taken into Paper 2 examinations, because of a belief that weaker candidates would spend too much time 'searching' it, the theory being that drama and poetry are more readily accessible.

4   During coursework assessment, an upward mark adjustment may be made in favour of first-year pieces of work.

5   Different institutions organise the work on extended essays in quite different ways. Some limit the content to 3 or 4 major fields; others offer a completely free choice. The most familiar pattern is for the essays to grow out of study of one of the texts studied elsewhere on the syllabus.

6   The final papers set are impressive evidence that this syllabus sets out to be scrupulously clear in its instructions. The gnomic questions familiar to some traditional syllabuses are replaced by very precise instructions.

Clearly these questions, which concentrate particularly on close commentary, have great influence on teaching styles. (See section on open book examinations.)

7   An evaluation of the 753 syllabus, which includes comparison with the 652 syllabus, is available from the Secretary of the board. This research is based on the 1979 candidature.

8   Termly standardisation/workshop meetings are *compulsory* (expenses being paid by LEA's).

2   JMB/SHEFFIELD

This syllabus combines 70% of the JMB set papers with 30% devised by the Sheffield consortium. Its most distinctive feature appears in its coursework element, in which there is a careful attempt to encourage different kinds of writing.

The syllabus is in addition to the JMB Shakespeare paper (Paper 1) without the long poem text and the JMB practical criticism paper (Paper 3). 20% of the whole A-level is based on the study of poetry and prose fiction texts selected by the consortium, and is assessed by means of a 2-hour open-book examination. The coursework accounts for 30% of the total and is arranged as follows. The folder contains 5 pieces of work from the whole course, 2 of which must come from the 'Wide Reading' section and the 'Composition' section. The other 3 may be drawn from the following sections – 'Composition', 'Drama', 'Poetry', 'Prose' or 'Optional subjects' (see below in Comments and Notes for details of this last option). There is a proviso that only 2 pieces may come from work in any one section. The normal maximum for each piece of work is 1500 words.

Quotation from the rubric for the 2 compulsory elements may be useful:

'Wide Reading
Candidates will submit a retrospective evaluation of what was interesting or significant in their reading . . . credit will be given for first-hand responses and knowledgeable interest . . . the writing submitted is likely to be different in kind from that submitted in other sections. The level of difficulty of the books will be taken into account.'
This piece may be either one 2000 work piece *or* 4 pieces (600 words) at the end of each of 4 terms.

Composition
Candidates . . . submit writing that demonstrates qualities accessible to others, without obscurity or private communing, with an awareness of audience, and an ability to adopt a variety of registers for different purposes. The work expected would be on a continuum from the narrative/descriptive to the reflective/analytical, i.e.
(i) personal writing – concerning personal experience, using the act of writing in verse or prose to distance and reshape this . . . demonstrating a capacity for drawing readers into a recreated world.
(ii) imaginative writing – writers seek by conventions of verse or prose fiction to explore and understand some aspect of human experience . . . to follow through the consequences of an imagined consistent world . . .
(iii) discursive writing – the writer may begin from a personal view . . .

the restrictions of a private viewpoint are admitted and attempts made to be objective. Such writing may be based on data presented for analysis.

Where verse is submitted, several poems may be offered up to a total of 50 lines as one piece of work.'

Particular stress is laid on the need for structure and form.

Breakdown of assessment	%
Papers 1 and 3 (board's own papers)	50
Paper 2 (externally-assessed open-book)	20
Coursework – 2 compulsory elements	12
3 optional elements	18
	100

Comments and notes

1   The Sheffield syllabus lays particular stress upon the language element in literature teaching – 'by this we do not mean linguistics, but the critical examination of writing skills and the application of such skills in the students' own work.' For this reason, they welcome the inclusion of more non-fictional prose in the board's practical criticism paper.

2   This same interest is reflected in the optional 'Optional Subjects' element of the coursework. This envisages work analysing the communication of opinion in writing or in speech, to concentrate on the methods of expression used, rather than on the opinion expressed. The language of persuasion is particularly cited as material for analysis.

3   There exists the possibility in the Drama option in the coursework for crossover with work done on the board's Paper 1. The same applies to the Prose option and the open-book Paper 2, although there is a stipulation that at least one extra text must be studied.

4   Because the Composition element is both a compulsory element, and a further optional element in the coursework, it is possible for this element to carry 12% of the total A-level marks.

5   As with the AEB/753, the value of consortium meetings is stressed.